First World War
and Army of Occupation
War Diary
France, Belgium and Germany

59 DIVISION
Headquarters, Branches and Services
Royal Army Veterinary Corps
Deputy Assistant Director Veterinary Services
9 February 1917 - 18 March 1919

WO95/3015/3

The Naval & Military Press Ltd
www.nmarchive.com
Published in association with The National Archives

Published by

The Naval & Military Press Ltd

Unit 10 Ridgewood Industrial Park,

Uckfield, East Sussex,

TN22 5QE England

Tel: +44 (0) 1825 749494

www.naval-military-press.com

www.nmarchive.com

This diary has been reprinted in facsimile from the original. Any imperfections are inevitably reproduced and the quality may fall short of modern type and cartographic standards.

© Crown Copyright
Images reproduced by permission of The National Archives, London, England, 2015.

Contents

Document type	Place/Title	Date From	Date To
Heading	WO 3015 59th Div Asst Div Veterinary Services 1917 Feb- 1919 Mar		
Heading	??		
Heading	Volume 2. 59th North Midland Division War Diary Assistant Director Of Veterinary Services. 59th Dv. February 1917		
War Diary	Fovant,	09/02/1917	23/02/1917
War Diary	Enroute	24/02/1917	26/02/1917
War Diary	Mericourt	27/02/1917	28/02/1917
Heading	Vol. 3. 59th North Midland Division. War Diary. Assistant Director of Veterinary Services. March 1917		
War Diary	Mericourt.	01/03/1917	09/03/1917
War Diary	Bois St Martin	10/03/1917	31/03/1917
War Diary	Mons Ec Chaussee	01/04/1917	11/04/1917
War Diary	Bouvincourt	12/04/1917	30/05/1917
War Diary	Equancourt.	31/05/1917	11/07/1917
War Diary	Barastre	12/07/1917	23/08/1917
War Diary	Achieux	24/08/1917	31/08/1917
War Diary	Winnizeele	01/09/1917	24/09/1917
War Diary	Brandhoek	25/09/1917	01/10/1917
War Diary	Steenbecque	02/10/1917	05/10/1917
War Diary	Bomy	06/10/1917	14/10/1917
War Diary	Chateau de-la Haie	15/10/1917	17/11/1917
War Diary	Hermaville	18/11/1917	19/11/1917
War Diary	Basseux.	20/11/1917	26/11/1917
War Diary	Etricourt.	27/11/1917	30/11/1917
War Diary	Vallulart Wood	01/12/1917	04/12/1917
War Diary	Little Wood	05/12/1917	14/12/1917
War Diary	Ytres	15/12/1917	22/12/1917
War Diary	Le Cauroy	23/12/1917	09/02/1918
War Diary	Gomiecourt	10/02/1918	11/02/1918
War Diary	Mory	12/02/1918	28/02/1918
War Diary	Behagnies	01/03/1918	21/03/1918
War Diary	Bucquoy	22/03/1918	22/03/1918
War Diary	Bouzincourt.	23/03/1918	24/03/1918
War Diary	Contay	25/03/1918	25/03/1918
War Diary	Fienvillers.	26/03/1918	27/03/1918
War Diary	Villers. Chatel	28/03/1918	28/03/1918
War Diary	Mingoval	29/03/1918	31/03/1918
War Diary	Couthove	01/04/1918	06/04/1918
War Diary	Brandhoek	07/04/1918	13/04/1918
War Diary	Boeschepe	14/04/1918	18/04/1918
War Diary	Couthove Chateau	19/04/1918	20/04/1918
War Diary	Vogeltje	21/04/1918	24/04/1918
War Diary	Bambecque	25/04/1918	25/04/1918
War Diary	Vogeltje	26/04/1918	30/04/1918
War Diary	Vogeltje	01/05/1918	06/05/1918
War Diary	St. Omer	07/05/1918	10/05/1918
War Diary	Eps.	11/05/1918	18/06/1918
War Diary	Bomy	19/06/1918	11/07/1918

War Diary	Monchy. Cayeux	12/07/1918	26/07/1918
War Diary	Basseux.	27/07/1918	23/08/1918
War Diary	Bavincourt.	24/08/1918	25/08/1918
War Diary	Norrent-Fontes	26/08/1918	27/08/1918
War Diary	Busnes	28/08/1918	06/09/1918
War Diary	St. Yenant	07/09/1918	07/09/1918
War Diary	Haystack Farm.	08/09/1918	10/09/1918
War Diary	Haystack Farm. Q.19.a.6.0 (36A)	10/09/1918	16/09/1918
War Diary	Haystack Farm.	16/09/1918	23/09/1918
War Diary	Farm. At R.14.a.9.9. (36 A)	24/09/1918	30/09/1918
War Diary	Farm R14.a.9.9. Ke Strenm.	01/10/1918	03/10/1918
War Diary	Estairs. L.22.C.6.3 (Sht 36 A)	04/10/1918	09/10/1918
War Diary	Bac. St. Maur.	10/10/1918	18/10/1918
War Diary	St Andre	19/10/1918	19/10/1918
War Diary	Hem. G 70.C.4.9 (37)	20/10/1918	20/10/1918
War Diary	Hem	21/10/1918	31/10/1918
War Diary	Sailly-Les-Lannoy	01/11/1918	08/11/1918
War Diary	Ramegnies Chin	09/11/1918	15/11/1918
War Diary	Wattignies	16/11/1918	05/12/1918
War Diary	Drouvin.	06/12/1918	07/12/1918
War Diary	Barlin	08/12/1918	24/12/1918
War Diary	Drouvin.	25/12/1918	07/03/1919
War Diary	Calais	08/03/1919	18/03/1919

WO 3015
59th Dn

Asst Dir Veterinary
Services

1917 Feb – 1919 Mar

Volume 2.

Secret

59th North Midland Division.

WAR DIARY.

Assistant Director of Veterinary Services. 59th Dv.

FEBRUARY 1917.

WAR DIARY or INTELLIGENCE SUMMARY

(Erase heading not required.)

A.D.V.S., 59th Div   February 1917.   Army Form C. 2118

Place	Date	Hour	Summary of Events and Information	Remarks and references to Appendices
Fovant,	9.2.17		Inspected horses of 177th Inty Bde. Clipping backward, 3 Units with no machines.	
,,	10.2.17		2/5th Sherwood F has no forge, no clipping machine heads, no lamps, no large mule shoes. Inspected 176th Bde. Codford, 2/5th N.S.Bn, Condition, shoeing, clipping, singeing, good. 2/6th S.S. Shoeing backward. 2/5th S.S Bn, Condition good, shoeing fair. 2/6th N.S. Conditin god. 514 Coy ASC, condition good, shoeing fair, 6 Lice cases.	
,,	11.2.17.		Visit to 515 and 516 Coys ASC and 3 newly arrived Machine Gun Coys, Condition fair.	
,,	13.2.17.		Inspection by H.M. THE KING.	
,,	14.2.17.		Visited D.DV.S S.C at SALISBURY.	
,,	15.2.17.		Inspected 1st and 2nd Field Ambls at Gillingham and 3rd at Shaftesbury with A.D.M.S.	
,,	16.2.17.		Visited CRA Larkhill. Interviewed Veterinary Officers.	
,,	17.2.17.		Visited 295th Bde and M.V.S and returned to FOVANT.	
,,	18.2.17 to 22.2.17.		Inspected all horses in FOVANT area prior to departure. Rendered Mange classification categories A.C.I 363 of 1916. to D.D.V.S Southern Command.	
En,route	23.2.17	10.30am.	Left FOVANT for SOUTHAMPTON.	
,,	24.2.17	12.30a.m.	Arrived LA HAVRE per S.S. Southwestern Miller. No casualties on board.	
,,	25.2.17	mmmm.	Entrained at le Havre for LONGEAU.	
,,	26.2.17	4.30	Arrived LONGEAU.	
MERICOURT	27.2.17.		Proceeded by route march to MERICOURT.arrived 6 p.m.	
,,	28.2.17		Opened A.D.V.S Office. Visited stables in district.	

Vol.3.

Secret.

59th North Midland Division.

WAR DIARY.

Assistant Director of Veterinary Services.

MARCH

1917.

Army Form C. 2118

WAR DIARY
or
INTELLIGENCE SUMMARY
(Erase heading not required.)

A.D.V.S.,

March 1917.

Instructions regarding War Diaries and Intelligence Summaries are contained in F.S. Regs., Part II and the Staff Manual respectively. Title Pages will be prepared in manuscript.

Place	Date	Hour	Summary of Events and Information	Remarks and references to Appendices
MERICOURT.	1.3.17.		Visited by D.D.V.S. Fourth Army.	
"	2.3.17.		Visited Longeau and Saleux re horses left behind by Units.5 horses at Orphanage, SALEUX had been evacuated by Fourth Army.1 horse left at M. Morel, Rue Nationale, LONGEAU. Wrote DDVS Fourth Army re this.	
"	4.3.17.		Visited 50th Div ADVS. Also inspected 50th Div M.V.A at R 27.c.	
"	5.3.17.		Inspected 513 Coy ASC, condition good except 5 horses in low condition, also 59th Div.Signal Coy RE Condition good, some have deteriorated in condition since leaving England.	
"	6.3.17.		A.S.C horses attached to D.H.Q have deteriorated during move.6 cases Pneumonia reported.	
"	7.3.17.		Visited D.D.V.S Fourth Army	
"	8.3.17		Went to PROVART with D.A.A.& Q.M.G re billets and stabling for M.V.S.Also inspected water troughs at Sugar Factory used by A.S.C and other Units.	
BOIS St MARTIN	9-3-17 10-3-17.		Moved by road to R 27. C 27. (dug outs) Inspected Transport en route. Advised DIVS change of location of Office of ADVS and of M.V.S to R 20 a 20. Reported Mange amongst horses of French roadmenders now using same troughs at R 20 c 20 as 59th Div.	
"	11-3.17		Inspected horses of 176th Bde, Field Coys RE, M.G.Coys and M.S.	
"	12-3-17		Inspected horses of 175th Bde. Visited sick horse left at MERICOURT. Called on ADVS 50th Div. Reported 7 horses killed 177th Machine Gun Coy by collapse of roof. Some horses of 177th Bde inspected. suspected case of Mange 513 Coy ASC. (not diagnosed).	
"	13.3.17.		Inspected horses of 177th Bde and M.G.C attached.Commended to Mallein horses of 59th Div.Train ASC consequent on instructions from DDVS Fourth Army to Mallein all horses in 59th Div.	
"	14.3.17 (to) 16.3.17		Inspected M.V.S horses?, with Sherwood F. and 2/5th S.F. Inspected Malleined horses Visited D OMG Hd Qtrs.	
"	17.3.17		Inspected malleined horses of of 467 Field Coy RE and 175th Machine G.Coys.Captain Bickerton AVC reported his arrival at HAMELET.	
"	18.3.17.		Visited D.D.V.S Fourth Army.	
"	19-3.17		Attended conference of A.D's V.S at QUERRIEUX.	
"	20.3.17		Inspected horses of 298th Bde RFA at CORBIE	
"	21.3.17.		Inspected horses of 176th Fifty Bde.All standing in open. Some few sinking in condition owing to exigencies of moment and inclement weather.Inspected 296th Bde RFA horses, interviewed O/C and informed him of extra ration of oats which can be demanded	
"	23-3.17		Inspected some horses of 298th Bde at CORBIE. Interviewed DVS Fourth Army	
"	24-3-17		Visited MV.S at PROVART. Saw horses of C Bty 296th Bde RFA. Many horses sinking in condition.	
"	25-3.17		Visited 298th Bde horses at Corbie. Horses in good condition with few exceptions.Inspected V.O;/c (Captain Conchie) to take veterinary charge of horses of 3rd Field Ambl at VILLERS-BRETO NEUX.	
"	26.3.17.		Inspected M.V.S horses for evacuation.Horse Ambl arrived but no harness or spare parts.	

Army Form C. 2118

A.D.V.S., March 17.

WAR DIARY
or
INTELLIGENCE SUMMARY
(Erase heading not required.)

Instructions regarding War Diaries and Intelligence Summaries are contained in F.S. Regs., Part II. and the Staff Manual respectively. Title Pages will be prepared in manuscript.

Place	Date	Hour	Summary of Events and Information	Remarks and references to Appendices
BOIS ST MARTIN	27.3.17		Inspected 3rd Field Ambl, VILLERS-BRETONNEUX. Found suspected case of Mange No 46 H.D. and instructed to send to M.V.S for evacuation.	
	28.3.17.		Visited MONS-EN-CHASSEE and saw horses of 470 Field Coy RE, 516 Coy ASC, A Bty 295th Bde RFA. Inspected M.V.S stables in afternoon.	
	29.3.17.		M.V.S moved from PROVART to MONS-EN-CHASSEE by march route via MISERY. Inspected horses of D.A.C. Reported loss of condition and number of deaths through exhaustion and excessive work to D.H.Q.	
	30.3.17.		Visited MONS-EN-CHASSEE and inspected horses of 196th Infantry Bde.	
	31-3-17.		Moved Office & ADVS to MONS-EN-C HASSEE. Notified DDVS change of location.	

Army Form C. 2118.

WAR DIARY
or
INTELLIGENCE SUMMARY

(Erase heading not required.)

Instructions regarding War Diaries and Intelligence Summaries are contained in F.S. Regs., Part II and the Staff Manual respectively. Title Pages will be prepared in manuscript.

A.D.V.S.
APRIL 1917

Place	Date	Hour	Summary of Events and Information	Remarks and references to Appendices
MORS EN CHAUSSÉE	1/4/17		At office of A.D.V.S.	
"	2/4/17		Inspected transport horses of 146 & 149 Brigade at Etrecourt.	
"	3/4/17		Isolated horses of 296 Brigade. No. 4103650 Gr. Y. Hancock transferred to 2/1 Mne. mob. Vet. Section.	
"	4/4/17		Saw horses for evacuation in M.V.S. Inspected Div. Train R.E. horses & reported to D.H.Q. and evacuated.	
"	5/4/17		Inspected Well C.R.A. horses of 295 Bde. R.F.A., 4 Lincs., 5 Leicester, Echelon B. D.A.C.	
"	6/4/17		Inspected 296 Bde. R.H.A. horses at Bouvincourt. Visited M.V.S. in afternoon.	
"	7/4/17		Inspected horses at Villers-Carbonnel. Reported to G.O.C. looking in condition of horses. D.A.C. Q.S.C. R.E. etc. of 91 Debility cases. 33 horses dead during week. 24 P.M.	
"	8/4/17		Inspected horses of Nd Tps 146 Bde. Leoncourt Farm. Reported condition to A.A.Q. horses sinking in condition 2 Kry Hus. 5 N.S.Bn., 6 N.S.Bn., 6 Sherwood Foresters Bn. 174 M.G. Coy. 467 Field Coy. R.E.	
"	9/4/17		Inspected horses 295 Bde. Reported to A.H.Q. & D.D.V.S. 4 Army. Approximately 150 Debilitated horses. Started to form Divisional Rest Camp for horses.	
"	10/4/17		Inspected 296 Bde. horses at Bouvincourt.	
"	11/4/17		Visited office of A.D.V.S. to 62 c.S.E. Edition 2A 9.23.B.5-9. Notified D.D.V.S. 4 Army.	
"	12/4/17		Visited M.V.S. Visited Bouchy with G.O.C. & R.R. Inspected horses 295 Bde. R.H.A.	
BOUVINCOURT	13/4/17		Inspected 4 Coys A.S.C. D.A.C. Echelon A. hutting of V.O.S	
"	14/4/17		Inspected 296 Bde. R.H.A. 3 Batteries under cover, 1 in open. Condition fair. 4 Debilitated horses evacuated to section. 4 sick, injured sent to section. 2 shrapnel cases. M.V.S. started horse rest camp. 62 sick & debilitated horses received first day. More to follow. Also inspected 469. M.G. Coy at Bouvincourt. Communicated with D.D.V.S. by telephone re debilitated horses.	

Army Form C. 2118.

WAR DIARY
or
INTELLIGENCE SUMMARY
(Erase heading not required.)

Instructions regarding War Diaries and Intelligence Summaries are contained in F. S. Regs., Part II. and the Staff Manual respectively. Title Pages will be prepared in manuscript.

ADVS II
APRIL 1917

Stamp: N.M. DIV — A.D.V.S. — 7 MAY 1917

Place	Date	Hour	Summary of Events and Information	Remarks and references to Appendices
BOUVINCOURT	15/4/17		Inspected 177 & 178 Bdes. & M.G. Section at Raisel	
"	16/4/17		Journeyed to H.Q. 4th Army & interviewed D.D.V.S. re Horse-wastage. Called at Toullay to inspect horses of 298 Bde. but found that the Bde. had left. Inspected sick lines of 3rd Field Ambulance.	
"	17/4/17		Sgt. Corbett. TT 03651 left for duty at No 2 Veterinary Hospital Havre.	
"			Inspected horses of 295 Bde. More horse becoming debilitated. 3 more dead chiefly owing to inclement weather last night. Nearly two Batteries under cover. Visited M.V.Sec. afternoon. A.D.M.S. examined water from ponds at Bouvincourt for inorganic poison. Results Nil.	
"			Interviewed G.O.C. re Debilitated horses.	
"	18/4/17		Inspected 176 Bde. 114th Field Coy & M.G. Coy. Majority of horses in fair condition. One or two horses in 5th & 6th South & 6th North Bde 176 Bde. commencing to get debilitated. 9 of the worst cases sent to Divisional Horse Rest Station. Several units shod with tin plate.	
"	19/4/17		Inspected horses 6th M.A. Gurneacourt Wood. 1 Debilitated horse in M.T.S.	
"	20/4/17		Inspected horse 4 Coys Q.S.C. & Debilitated horse of A.D.C. Condition improving. Conference of V.O.s	
"			Inspected Malleined horses of 5th N.J. No reaction.	
"	21/4/17		Inspected horses of 296 Bde 144 M.G. Coy & 469 Coy R.E at Bouvincourt. Inspected 177 Bde in company with Col. Hazelrigg. O.c. Div Train. Horses of 5th Lines & Bde H.Q. poor in condition. Capt Paley. left for 10 days rest.	
"	22/4/17		Inspected condition good. Contagious disease.	
"	23/4/17		Inspected horses of 1st Field Ambulance. Echelon A.D.A.C. & legal Coy R.E. Inspected horses of 295 Bde. 60% of horse rather low in condition. Stable management improved since last week. Inspected horses of 4th Lincolns. in company with Divisional Train.	

WAR DIARY or INTELLIGENCE SUMMARY

Army Form C. 2118.

ADVS
APRIL 1917

Place	Date	Hour	Summary of Events and Information	Remarks and references to Appendices
BOUVINCOURT	24/4/17		Inspected horses of 469 Coy R.E. about 8 horses in poor condition. 175 Mach Gun Coy. All horses in good condition. 5th Norwood Dorsets had case of "licked up Nail" horses in good condition. 1st Norwood Dorsets horses good condition. D Battery 296 Bde. 2 horses evacuated several horses poor stable management. Very weak mile Arty. Inspected debilitated horses at Gouzeaucourt Wood condition improving.	
"	25/4/17		Inspected horses of D.A.C. Cartigny. Number of thin mules in Echelon A. Rumours on cooked food. Several treatment not worthwhile. 200 Mach. Gun. Coy. Bennet, 1 thin horse. Remainder horses mule in good condition. Visited M.V.S. 40 horses in Rest Camp. Sick line mostly debility cases. Latter improving.	
"	26/4/17		Accompanied D.D.V.S. on inspection of Div. train. M.V.S. Div Horse Rest Camp & D.A.C. debility cases. Visited 296 Bde R.F.A. sick line	
"	27/4/17		Inspected horses of 144 Brigade with D.A. Q.M.G. Conference of I.O's.	
"	28/4/17		Inspected horses of C.296 Brigade. Condition better. 2 cases of suspected mange discovered. Sent to M.V.S. Visited M.V.S. Horse Rest Camp. Debilitated horses improving.	
"	29/4/17		Inspected horses of 295 Brigade. 4 evacuated 3 debility cases & 1 mare for foal. Inspected horses of Headquarters 144 Brigade. Evacuated 2 debility cases & 1 P.U.N. Inspected horses of 5th Lincs. 1 Cellulitis case evacuated. Condition improving.	
"	30/4/17		Inspected horses of D.A.C. at Cartigny & shows thin horses which have been received from 295 Brigade. About 80 horses on Horse Rest Lines at home very thin & debilitated & 120. at Cartigny. Very thin & low in condition	

WAR DIARY or INTELLIGENCE SUMMARY

59 Div. A.D.V.S.

MAY 1917

Army Form C. 2118. — 7 JUN 1917 — 59th (N.M.) DIVIS.

Place	Date	Hour	Summary of Events and Information	Remarks and references to Appendices
Bouzincourt	1/5/17		Inspected horses of 5th South Staffs. Engineers & Mach Gun Coy at Berno. A.Q. 174 Bde & 5th Notts & thin horses noting & grazing as much as possible. 4th Lincs 6 thin horses unable to rest. Gun, grazing as much as possible. A.Q. 178 Bde horses looking very poor.	Vet 4
"	2/5/17		Inspected horses of 178 Inf Bde. Mach Gun Coy Engineers at Roisel & thin horses in 5th Bn Sherwood Foresters. Condition of 5th Sherwood Foresters very good. Mach Gun mules & weazen iced. Condition of all horses improving. 1 serious case of "Picked up Nail". Shoeing with new plate material not good enough. Visited Sick line 296 Bde. Mach Gun R.E. at Bouzincourt.	
"	3/5/17		Attended conference. A.D.V.S. of Army. Inspected horses Mob Vet Section & 2nd Field Ambulance. Latter rather loose in condition but improving.	
"	4/5/17		A.I.C. visited Sick lines of all 4 Coys Thin horses improving, some showing marked change in the better. Conference of V.O's. Demonstration with choke helmets for horses, & arrangements made with Capt Dawes Gas Officer to give demonstration to Officers & N.C.O's of 1st Line transport.	
"	5/5/17		R.A.C. Echelon B. Inspected 139 horses in low condition, received from R.A. 'Debilitated' horses to be evacuated through 42nd M.V.S. Inspected D Bty. 296 Bde & gave instruction for 4 horses. 2 debility & ignition to be evacuated. Some horses low in condition.	
"	6/5/17		Inspected horses A.H.Q, M.M.P, & 59th Div Signal. Mob Vet Section 8 bad foot cases result of Picked up Nail. Div Horse Rest camp. 24 horses returned to duty 6 debility cases orders into M.V.S. for evacuation. Inspected sick line 296 Bde R.F.A.	
"	7/5/17		A.D.V.S. 4th Army inspected Horse Rest Camp & H.V.S. also D.A.C. Echelon B. thin horses. Inspected horses of M.V.S. for evacuation.	

WAR DIARY
or
INTELLIGENCE SUMMARY

(Erase heading not required.)

Instructions regarding War Diaries and Intelligence Summaries are contained in F. S. Regs., Part II. and the Staff Manual respectively. Title Pages will be prepared in manuscript.

A.D.M.S. II
MAY 1914

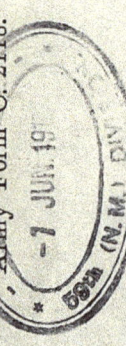

Place	Date	Hour	Summary of Events and Information	Remarks and references to Appendices
BOURLINCOURT	8/5/19		Inspected horses of 174 Bde. "Divisional Grenade Dump. Called on O.C. D.A.C. & Divisional Forester of this horse with him.	
	9/5/19		Attended sick line. 295 Bde R.F.A. Instructed V.O. to evacuate 2 horses - (debility & cellulitis). Inspected horses 5th, 6th, 8th Sherwood Foresters. Condition of horses improving. Inspected whole of Div. Train. 29 sick horses have been put to light duties. Report to be sent to D.A.D.V.S. suggesting further rest & treatment.	
	10/5/19		Inspected horses 2nd Field Ambulance, sick lines B & C Batteries 295 Bde. Inspected horses D Battery 295 Bde & evacuated 1 (foaling mare, debility). 1 kick on stifle to M.V.S. Base Hospital. Visited M.V.S. arranged for evacuation. Capt Morley D.V.S. reported for duty. Visited 6. 296 Bde R.F.A.	
	11/5/19		Visited M.V.S. Conference of Veterinary Officers	
	12/5/19		Inspected horses D.A.C. & 296 S.do R.F.A.	
	13/5/19		Inspected sick horses of D.A.C. at above. Divisional signal Condition improving Capt Rickerton "Ca." Officer gave demonstration to Sherwood Foresters on use of Va. Velvetofolio.	
	14/5/19		Inspected horses of 295 Bde. 1st Sherwood Foresters & M.V.S. D.A.D.V.S. 4th Army called & looked at horses of D.A.C.	
	15/5/19		Inspected horses of 174 Bde. Horses of 5 M Coy R.E. much improved in condition. 174 M.G. Coy. 1 very lame. 174 M.G. Coy. 1 Bad case of Ophthalmia in mule. 414 Field Coy animals in good condition.	
	16/5/19		Inspected horses of 178 Inf Bde & M.V.S.	
	17/5/19		D.D.V.S. visited the V.S. B & C. Batteries 296 Bde. horses of A & D batteries in fair condition. Inspected horses of Div. Train 5th & 6th Sherwood Foresters 2 thin horses in 2/5 Bn.	

WAR DIARY or INTELLIGENCE SUMMARY

A.D.V.S. III
MAY 1917

Place	Date	Hour	Summary of Events and Information	Remarks and references to Appendices
BOUVINCOURT.	18/5/17		Interviewed C.R.A. Conference of V.Os. Inspected horse of Div. Train 9 thin horses but improved since last week	
"	19/5/17		Inspected horse Echelon B.A.C. sent 5 thin horses to M.V.S. for evacuation. Remainder of sent improving. Horses fit for service. Visited M.V.S. & inspected horses for evacuation. Inspected horses of 4th Bty. R.H.A. 148 Bde.	
"	20/5/17		Visit of acting A.D.V.S. Inspected horses of 295 Bde. respecting outbreak of stomatitis. Also 3 horse 5th Lincs.	
"	21/5/17		Inspected horses 295 Rde. Visited M.V.S. Demonstration 147 Bde on use of Helnets for horses.	
"	22/5/17		Examined injured horse. Signal Section. Ordered destruction (severed tendon)	
"	23/5/17		Inspected horses 148 Bde. Gun condition practically no sick. Called on A.D.V.S. 40th Division re horse	
"	24/5/17		Mobile Veterinary Section	
"	25/5/17		Visited new area with C.R.E. Conference of V.Os.	
"	26/5/17		Inspected horses of D.A.C. Signal Section & Remounts	
"	27/5/17		Visited new area, M.V.S.	
"	28/5/17		Called on A.D.V.S. 2nd Cav. Division. Visited M.V.S.	
"	29/5/17		Rang up A.D.V.S. 4th Army re inspection for mange of London & 110 Heavy Btys. N.C.R. Inspected 147 In G. Coy. & H.Q. 176 Bde.	
EQUANCOURT.	30/5/17		Moved office to Equancourt.	
"	31/5/17		Arranging new locations for M.V.S. Reports verbally to A.D.V.S. case of mange in 178 Tunnelling Coy. 42 in Division	

J. Millward Capt.
A.V.C.

Army Form C. 2118.

WAR DIARY
or
INTELLIGENCE SUMMARY

(Erase heading not required.)

JUNE 1917 Vol 5

A.D.V.S. 1 JUL 1917 189th (N.M.) DIVISION

Instructions regarding War Diaries and Intelligence Summaries are contained in F.S. Regs., Part II. and the Staff Manual respectively. Title Pages will be prepared in manuscript.

Place	Date	Hour	Summary of Events and Information	Remarks and references to Appendices
EQUANCOURT	June 1st		Met 1st section moving. Inspected Brigadier horse 176 Brigade. Inspected horses of 11 London & 110 Battery R.G.A. & reported mange to D.D.V.S.	
	2nd		Off 2nd Field Amb. Interviewed A.D.V.S. 40th Division arranged inspection of mange cases for D.D.V.S. of D.A.C. section & 11 London & 110 R.G.A.	
	4th		Inspected horses of D.A.C. section in this area. No sick. All animals in good condition. 176 Bde. with 2 exceptions all animals in good condition. Same case. 174 M.G. Coy. 4th Leicesters several thin horse. D.D.V.S. inspected skin	
	5th		cases of 4 Heavy Battery R.G.A. Inspected horses of 178 Bde. very few sick. H.Q. 3 thin horse. Arranged to transport of sick from Heavy Artillery. Gave auto gas demonstration to officers M.E.O.S. 176 Bde. D.A.C. & R.E.	
	6th		Discovered 1 case stomatitis in H.Q. 176 Bde. Telephoned D.D.V.S.	
	7th		Visited M.V.S. arranged for N.C.O. to accompany horse to Base Hospital with Moto. Ambulance. Inspected horses 3rd Field Amb. horses not looking so well in condition 1 mare heavy in foal sent to M.V.S. for evacuation	
	8th		Attended Board Consisting A.D.V.S. 40th & 59th Divisions & Corps. R.E. Officer to locate site for Baths. for horses of Heavy battery with division with division.	
	9th		Inspected horse 176 & 147 Brigade horses of 4th June & 4 & 5 Leicesters have fallen away in condition somewhat. Judged horse at show of 176 Bde.	
	10th		Inspected horses of 3 Field Coy. R.E. Let 3 lame horse to M.V.S. Inspected horse of D.H.Q. & M.M.P. with suspected skin. Also Div. Signal Coy. Condition good.	
	11th		R.G.A. met Capt Ryan A.M.S. Reported absence of grooming kit, water trough, & clipping machine to D.D.V.S. & inspected horse of D.A.C. held outbreak of Stomatitis	
	12th		110 Heavy Battery. Inspected for mange. 115 & 125 Batt. & accompanied 1/c 155 Batt. Capt Bradley A.V.C. reported for duty.	

WAR DIARY
or
INTELLIGENCE SUMMARY

Army Form C. 2118.

JUNE 1917

Place	Date	Hour	Summary of Events and Information	Remarks and references to Appendices
EQUANCOURT	June 13		Inspected 1/1 London Bty. R.G.A. & suggested speeding up treatment of mange case. Met A.D.V.S. re defying bath for horses. Called on O Office III Corps. re pecting supply of Ordnance Stores	
"	14		also interviewed D.A.D.O.S. 59th Divn. re pecting same. Visited sick line of 3rd & 6th Sault Staff	
"	15th		Inspected horses 155 Battery R.G.A. for skin disease. Inspected horses 178 Bde. with O.C. Des Band	
"			horses in very good condition. Visited M.V.S. re evacuation	
"	16th		1st & 2nd Field Amb. Condition good. No sick	
"	17th		Inspected N.Q. horses & M.M.P. also gas demonstration to same. Inspected signallers & sick lines	
"			118 Brigade Sports	
"	18th		Inspected horses 5 Batts. R.G.A. & 3 Corps R.E.	
"	19th		Inspected sick horselines of R.G.A. Horse shown afternoon 148 Bde.	
"	20th		Inspected 110th/155 v/r Kent Batts. R.G.A. Visited Q Officer Corps H.Q. re supply stable equipment	
"	21st		Visited M.I.S.	
"	22nd		Inspected horses of 115 Battery R.G.A.	
"	23rd		" " 125 " " Conference of V.O.'s	
"	24th		" " 155 " " Returned 93 horses to duty	
"			" 3 Corps R.E. & signallers. Inspected mobile Vet Section	
"	25th		110 Battery R.G.A. & visited horses in good condition. Inspected horses.	
"			met A.D.V.S. 4th Army & A.D.V.S. III Corps. & inspected 1/1 London Battery R.G.A. for mange.	
"			Inspected 1/1 Kent Battery R.G.A. for skin disease. Cease sinkrotic mange in latter	
"			" horses of Div Train. Condition good.	
"	26th		Inspected horses of 146, 147 & 148 Inf Bde. All animals in good condition. Very few minor injuries.	

Army Form C. 2118.

WAR DIARY
or
INTELLIGENCE SUMMARY
(Erase heading not required.)

Instructions regarding War Diaries and Intelligence Summaries are contained in F. S. Regs., Part II. and the Staff Manual respectively. Title Pages will be prepared in manuscript.

JUNE 1917

Place	Date	Hour	Summary of Events and Information	Remarks and references to Appendices
EQUANCOURT.	June 27th		Inspected horses of 2nd & 3rd Field Ambulances. All horses in working condition. Also inspected grazing grounds of Heavy Batteries R.G.A. Sent report to A.D.V.S. III Corps.	
	28		Number of horses evacuated for mange since his inspection. Inspected horses 115 & 125 Batteries R.F.A. for skin disease. None of 1/1 London Battery that have been mallened.	
	29		Examined horses 1/1 London. About 6 fresh cases. Twelve sick being 110 Heavy Battery R.G.A. Examined Mallened horses 155 Battery. Mallein test for 1/1 London 110 & 155 Heavy Batteries sent to III Corps. No reactors. Urgea spots My Brigade.	
	30		Inspected horses 155 Battery for skin disease & glanders.	

J. William Eve
Major A.V.C.

Army Form C. 2118.

WAR DIARY
or
INTELLIGENCE SUMMARY
(Erase heading not required.)

D.A.D.V.S.
JULY 1917

Place	Date	Hour	Summary of Events and Information	Remarks and references to Appendices
EQUANCOURT	July 1st		Accompanied D.A.Q.M.G. to remount Depot of the Army, to select remounts	
"	2nd		Inspected range lines of London 115 Heavy Battery R.G.A. The remounts in all 5 Heavy Batteries 15. Suspicious Skin. 1 Remount in 115 Battery destroyed for injured back. Inspected horses 200 Mach Gun Coy. Condition good. Visited M.V.S. Re evacuation of horses.	
"	3rd		Visited Army Headquarters. Examined remounts with D.A.Q.M.G. Attended Div train 6.30pm to see Remounts. Inspected mange lines 110, 125 & 155 Heavy Batteries	
"	4th		Visited horse line Div train Re distribution of remounts. Visited M.V.S.	
"	5th		Inspected horses D.G.C. condition good. Inspected horses of 125 & 115 Heavy Batteries.	
"	6th		Inspected horses of 1st London Heavy Battery evacuated 1 Saresophic care Inspected horse of 176 Brigade Headquarters & Visited M.V.S.	
"	7th		Attended conference A.D.V.S. 3rd Corps. Inspected horses 155 Heavy	
"	8th		Inspected horses Div Head Quarters & visited M.V.S.	
"	9th		Visited M.V.S. & Inspected sick lines of 1st London 110 & 155 Heavy Batteries. Capt Dooly proceeded 14 days leave.	
"	10th		Proceeded with A.Q.G. to select site for M.V.S. Arranged for Transport of M.V.S. Pte Earp M.V.S. proceeded 10 days leave.	
"	11th		M.V.S. moved 54c O2y M central Office moved 54c O15 A central Visited Heavy Batteries & 3rd Corps Headquarters.	
BARASTRE	12th		Visited 1st London, 115, 125 & 155 Heavy Batteries, R.G.A. in company with A.D.V.S. 3rd Army. A.D.V.S. 3rd Corps & A.D.V.S. 4th Corps in connection with outbreak of mange in these units.	
"	13th		Visited M.V.S. Inspected horses of A.S.C. & 200 Mach Gun Coy.	
"	14th		Conference A.D.V.S. 4th Corps. Visited M.V.S. & Mob. Veterinary meeting. Capt Morley to proceed to duty with 1st King Edwards Horse. Capt Bradley with 296 Bde R.F.A.	
"	15th		Visited M.V.S. Inspected horse lines, sick lines, mens billets etc. Visited Exercise "Inspected Gen Jaure injured horse. left there. Inspected horses of Div Headquarters	

2449 Wt. W14957/M90 750,000 1/16 J.B.C. & A. Forms/C.2118/12.

WAR DIARY or INTELLIGENCE SUMMARY

D.A.D.V.S.
JULY. 1917.

Army Form C. 2118.

Place	Date	Hour	Summary of Events and Information	Remarks and references to Appendices
BARASTRE	July 16/17		Visited M.V.S. Inspected sick lines of Stafford. Sherwood Foresters & 200 Mach Gun Coy.	
	17th		Inspected horses of D.A.C.	
			Visited M.V.S. evacuated 2 truck loads of horses. Inspected horses of 174 Inf Bde Mach Gun Coy.	
	18th		Field Coy R.E.	
			Visited M.V.S. Inspected horses of S.A.A. Section D.A.C. Superintended firing of fences for sheds.	
	19th		Div Horse Show	
	20th		Inspected cases in M.V.S. & horses of 146 Bde & Mach Gun Coy & 2/3 Field Amb. Condition fair	
	21st		Attended Conference A.D.V.S. IV Corps. Inspected horses of 1st Field Amb. evacuated 2 cases	
			of suspected mange. Arranged for horses to be dressed c Elipsen etc.	
			Visited Headquarters 40th Division Interviewed D.A.D.V.S. re horses to 296 Bde & D.A.C.	
			Called & walked round lines of 296 Bde. Visited M.V.S.	
	22nd		Inspected horses, saddlery, uniforms etc of M.V.S. Inspected sick lines 178 Inf Bde & Mach Gun Coy.	
			D.A.C. All minor injuries	
	23rd		Inspected horses of A.S.C. Visited M.V.S.	
	24th		Visited M.V.S. Capt Tooley returned from leave	
	25th		Major Coe proceeded for leave Capt Tooley takes over duties	
			Visited 178 Inf Bde. S.A.A. Section D.A.C. 178 Mach Gun Coy. #469 Field Coy R.E.	
	26th		M.V.S. & 178 Bde.	
	27th		M.V.S. & Visited 2/1 Field Amb. at Nivolani. #469 Field Coy R.E.	
	28th		M.V.S. & Attended Conference A.D.V.S. IV Corps.	
	29th		M.V.S.	
	30th		Inspected M.V.S. 146 Bde. 174 Bde. 200 Mach Gun Coy 446 Field Coy R.E. with	
			A.D.V.S. IV Corps.	
	31st		M.V.S. & Inspected 178 Bde. with A.D.V.S. IV Corps. & 4th Corps.	

Guy G. Scott
Capt for major D.V.S.

CONFIDENTIAL **WAR DIARY** *or* **INTELLIGENCE SUMMARY**

(Erase heading not required.)

Army Form C. 2118.

D.A.D.V.S.
AUGUST 1917.

Instructions regarding War Diaries and Intelligence Summaries are contained in F.S. Regs., Part II and the Staff Manual respectively. Title Pages will be prepared in manuscript.

Place	Date	Hour	Summary of Events and Information	Remarks and references to Appendices
Beaumetz	August 1st		M.V.S.&Visited A.S.C.attached 295 Brigade at Hamelet.	
	2nd		M.V.S.&Inspected horses of 1st Field Ambulance at Moislains.	
	3rd		M.V.S.	
	4th		M.V.S. Attended Conference A.D.V.S.IV.Corps.	
	5th		M.V.S. Inspected horses of 178 Inf.Brigade.470Field Coy.R.E.175 Machine Gun Coy.&S.A.A.Section.D.A.C.	
	6th		M.V.S.&D.H.Q.	
	7th		M.V.S.& Inspected horses of 200 Machine Gun Coy.&469 Field Coy.R.E.	
	8th		M.V.S.& Inspected 1stLine Transport of 176 & 177 Inf. Brigades.	
	9th		M.V.S.& Inspected horses of 1st Field Ambulance. Major J.W.Coe returned from leave.	
	10th		Visited M.V.S. Inspected horses of 178Inf. Brigade & 175 Machine Gun Coy.	
	11th		Inspected Sick Lines of Staffords.	
	12th		Inspected horses of M.M.P.&D.H.Q. Inspected 3 Coys of R.E's in company with C.R.E.for repatriation of mares re Divisional Circular No271.	
	13th		Inspected horses of 1st Field Ambulance. Some looking thin. One case of mange left.	
	14th		Inspected horses of 59th Divisional Train.	
	15th		Visited M.V.S. Inspected horses of 178 Inf. Brigade.(Judged sports of 176 Inf. Brigade.)	
	16th		Visited M.V.S. Capt.H.W.Dawes proceeded on leave.	
	17th		Visited M.V.S. with D.A.D.V.S.3rd Division re Gas Chamber for horses. Inspected horses of 178Inf.Bde.	
	18th		Inspectetd Brood Mares of 295 & 296 Brigades R.F.A.with C.R.A.	
	19th		Attended Conference A.D.V.S.IV Corps. Major J.W.Coe injured,Capt.G.Sooby took over duties.	
			M.V.S. Inspected horses of 176 Inf. Brigade & Machine Gun COY. 177 Inf. Brigade. 200 Machine Gun Coy. 469 Field Coy R.E. & 467 Field Coy RE.	
	20th		M.V.S. Inspected horses of 2/2nd Field Ambulance, 178 Inf. Brigade &59th Divisional Train A.S.C.	
	21st		M.V.S. Inspected horses of 467,469,470 Field Coys R.E. 2/5th South Staffs & 2/1st Field Ambulance.	
	22nd		M.V.S. & 4th Corps Cyclists.	
	23rd		Moved Office to Achieux. Map reference 57D.S.E.Pl3A.central.	
Achieux.	24th		Moved M.V.S. to Bouzincourt. Map reference 57D.SE.W7 central. Inspected horses of 2/6 South Staffs.	
	25th		M.V.S. Visited 178 Brigade,No.4.Coy A.S.C, 175 Machine Gun Coy&2/6 South Staffords.	
	26th		M.V.S. Visited 2/5 & 2/6 North Staffords & 469 Field Coy R.E.	
	27th		M.V.S. Visited 176 Brigade & No.3.Coy A.S.C. Picking out mares. Capt Bright A.V.C. arrived to take over duties of D.A.D.V.S.	
	28th		Visited M.v.S.	
	29th		Visited M.v.S. Inspected horses of 1st Field Ambulance & Divisional Headquarters.	
	30th		"Divisional Train	
	31st		Moving Office.	

2449 Wt. W14957/M90 750,000 1/16 J.B.C. & A. Forms/C.2118/12.

L.Fletcher
Capt. A.V.C.
DADVS 59th

WAR DIARY
or
INTELLIGENCE SUMMARY

(Erase heading not required.)

Army Form C. 2118.

Instructions regarding War Diaries and Intelligence Summaries are contained in F.S. Regs., Part II. and the Staff Manual respectively. Title Pages will be prepared in manuscript.

Stamp: A.D.V.S. - 2 OCT 1917 59th (N.M.) DIVISION

Place	Date	Hour	Summary of Events and Information	Remarks and references to Appendices
WINNIZEELE	10/21/1st		Moving office to S.N.A.4.4. Vieet 24.	
"	2nd		Visited N.V.S. & A.D.V.S. XIX Corps.	
"	3rd		Inspected horses of 200 Mach. Gun Coy, 469 Field Coy, No 1 Coy A.S.C., 178 Inf. Bde & 175 M.G. Coy.	
"	4th		" 174 Inf Bde, 3 Coys Div. Train, 179 M.G. Coy.	
"	5th		" 2/2 & 2/3 Field Ambulances. 295 Bde R.F.A. & D.A.C.	
"	7th		" 1/1 175 Machine Gun Coy & inspected unit. Lt Col Hazebury 1st Line Transport	
"	8th		of 176, 177 & 178 Inf Bde.	
"	9th		Inspected horses of 476 Field Coy R.E. Visited Advanced Remount Section.	
"	10th		Attended conference A.D.V.S. & D.D.V.S. Flowry.	
"	11th		Visited N.V.S. Inspected horses of 2/2/1 Field Ambulance.	
"	12th		D.H.Q.	
"	13th		Inspected 2/6 N Staff & dudged transport officers re care of their animals. Inspected H.Q. Signal recommended 3 horses for evacuation. Inspected 2 Coys Div. Train. Visited Nº1 Sick Horse Halt to arrange re evacuation.	
"	14th		Inspected 476 Coy R.E., N.Q. 174 Inf Bde. I.D.H.Q. Notice many units are not inspected for sufficient frequent enough. Attention of H.Q. drawn to matter via notice in orders re keep in untage.	
"	15th		Inspected horse for evacuation at N.V.S.	
"	16th		Attended conference A.D.V.S. V Corps re discus arrangement for evacuation. Returned via Bde location of N.V.S. etc in event of moving to forward area. Examined Remount & arrived to H.Q. Examined Major Ridley's charger.	
"	17th		Inspected all animals 175, 177, 200 Machine Gun Coy. 174 Coy has one sick mule & talk would do so back so very weak. Examined Major Ridley charger refused its stable.	
"	18th		Inspected with Capt Daug. N.Q. Signal recommended our horse sick mule to be cast & all 174 Bde. Recommended an animal & Veterinary Ravon. Inspected 2 Coy A.S.C. all 174 Bde. Recommended an animal & Equestrian to be cast for Veterinary Ravon. Major Ridley Charger.	
"	19th		Inspected horses 1/6 Inf Bde. Visited N.V.S.	

Army Form C. 2118.

WAR DIARY
or
INTELLIGENCE SUMMARY.
(Erase heading not required.)

Instructions regarding War Diaries and Intelligence Summaries are contained in F. S. Regs., Part II. and the Staff Manual respectively. Title pages will be prepared in manuscript.

D.A.D.V.S.
2 OCT 1917
59th (N.M.) DIVISION

Place	Date	Hour	Summary of Events and Information	Remarks and references to Appendices
WINNIZEELE	Sept 20		Inspected horses of 177 Bde. v B.H.Q.	
"	21		" " 178 " Visited M.V.S.	
"	22		Attended Conference ADVS F Corps.	
"	23		Visited H.Q. 55th Division to arrange for taking over. Visited 55th Div M.V.S. with Capt Cooley.	
BRANDHOEK	24		Arrived H.Q. D.M.S. & Branched. Visited M.V.S.	
"	25		Visited H.Q. D.A. Train & M.V.S. Inspected horses 296 Bde R.F.A. Mounting of Col's Batteries very bad. Reported on same. M.V.S. evacuated 34 Road & 35 times over. Left behind Maj 55 Divn.	
"	26		Visited M.V.S. to arrange re evacuation. Inspected Wagon Line of 295 Bde R.F.A. v D.A.C. arranged for attendance of 6 men to M.V.S. to assist in dealing with cases in M.V.S.	
"	27		Inspected horses of 467, 469, 470 Field Cos. R.E. v R.H.Q.	
"	28		Visited M.V.S. Visited horse dep on Poperinghe Smith Road.	
"	29		Attended several horse casualties among Signal, 469 & 470 Field Cos.	
"	30		Visited advanced Veterinary Aid Posts of 59th & 3rd Divisions. M.V.S. & Divisional Train.	
"			Visited M.V.S. to arrange re evacuation on morning.	

W.F.Morgan
Major A.V.C.

WAR DIARY or INTELLIGENCE SUMMARY

(Erase heading not required.)

D.A.D.V.S.
59th Division
October 1914

Place	Date	Hour	Summary of Events and Information	Remarks and references to Appendices
BRAND HOEK	1-10-17		Met A.D.V.S. NZ Division & conducted him to Advanced Rest Post & M.V.S. explaining Veterinary arrangements in area of Division & system of evacuation via Railway by road to St OMER von dep specially notified by Corps. At WIPPENHOEK (Train Cage) drew his attention to the urgent need for the provision by unit of more protection for horse against bombs.	
STEENBECQUE	2-10-17		NZ.M.V.S. arrived & worked in conjunction with 2/1 M.M.V.S. sharing Billets moved office to STEENBECQUE Removal now complete. Change location of M.V.S. & M.V.S. arrives with exception of 1 N.C.O. & men to proceed to St OMER. 1/c Road Case. Capt Bickerton A.V.C. 10.295 Bde proceed on own.	
"	3-10-17		Visited M.V.S. and that the total casualties from bomb shell about during 8 days in the line of V.P.R.F.S. Salient amount to 43% of war that horse strength (including artillery) that the number killed or destroyed during this period amounted to 23% from this cause. Most casualties were about 3 lost & 3 shell. The lost casualties are to a considerable extent preventable by a 4ft wall of dung stack or sandbags & a lot more of such provision is necessary in this area. Evacuation from M.V.S. are now by Road to St OMER.	
"	4-10-17		Inspected 174 Bde Area. Horses are mostly in open & are suffering lately from continuous rain	
"	5-10-17		Division in process of move to BOMY area.	
BOMY	6-10-17		Moved with B.H.Q. to BOMY M.V.S. moved to RUPIGNY	
	7-10-17		Visited M.V.S. at RUPIGNY. On arrival of M.V.S. at B.H.Q. previous evening no billets had been allotted them in their area. & as other units were allotted the same area they had difficulty in finding a location & Men & Horses were in a very unsuitable one for M.V.S. without water for men or horses. Reported circumstances to B.H.Q. with view to better billeting arrangements	
	8-10-17		Visited units in 174 Bde area. After 4 days rain standing for horses mostly in open are in a very bad condition	
	9-10-17		Capt R.W. Baynes A.V.C. moves out of area with Dirt Train. Inspected unit M.V.S. at Lores of 2/4 Notts Derby: Here are a number beginning to lose condition. Reported this fact to B.H.Q. & asked their assistance to procure safer Stores & chaff cutters to assist unit who require it to provide boiled feed for such animals & learnt that stoves are on order & chaff cutters should be provided in new area.	
	10-10-17		Inspected 4 animals in 59 Sig Coy unfit to march. arranged with 2nd Army M.O. for the provision of motor ambulance to evacuate them to St OMER.	
	11-10-17		Inspected H.Q. of M.V.S. Remainder of Division in process of moving	
	12-10-17		Visited M.V.S.	

WAR DIARY
or
INTELLIGENCE SUMMARY.
(Erase heading not required.)

Instructions regarding War Diaries and Intelligence Summaries are contained in F.S. Regs., Part II. and the Staff Manual respectively. Title pages will be prepared in manuscript.

Army Form C. 2118

D.A.D.V.S.
59th (N.M.) Division

Place	Date	Hour	Summary of Events and Information	Remarks and references to Appendices
BOMY.	13-10-17.		M.V.S. moved to Bomy. All transport is now out of Divisional area.	
"	14-10-17		Moved office to Chateau-de-la-HAIE. Visited location of M.V.S. at PETIT SERVINS. The location is a good one conveniently near transport line of unit. Standings good & protection from wind & rain can be easily arranged. Accommodation for men also good. Standing for about 50 horses & an isolation line. M.V.S. arrived at PETIT SERVINS.	
CHATEAU-de-la-HAIE	15-10-17		Visited Corps H.Q. & discussed veterinary arrangements for the area with A.D.V.S. Corps. Evacuation from BARLIN can be arranged with R.T.O. any day. Visited BOUVIGNY & inspected and the possible M.V.S. site. The location standing & accommodation are very good but the present location of M.V.S. is more convenient. There is a horse dip at BARLIN for this Coup.	
"	16-10-17		Visited M.V.S. arranged with O.C. to carry out improvements to flooring, to provide wind & rain protection &c. Arranged with C.R.E. with reference to provision of material. Attended trapping parade of brood mares with Corps Horsemaster & DAD XIII Corps.	
"	17-10-17		Visited M.V.S. Inspected with O.C. Div Train. Horses of A.V.Q. & M.M.P. Draworks standings & location of Bde Transport. Standings are generally very good well protected. Inspected with O.C. Div Train 1/5 M.G. Coy, Condition good;	
"	18-10-17		2/4 Field Amb. Condition fairly good, evacuated 1 H/D for debility. Order 4 or 5 annual losing condition to receive special treatment. Suggested to A.D.M.S. that this & 2/4 & 2/3 F.A.s provide wheel clipping machine out of their funds. 1/5 Sherwood. Condition good, standing requires repairs, evacuated 1 H.D. with chronic laminitis. 2/6 Sherwood. Condition good standing requires repair, arranges for provision of water trough. Stand bucket. 2/6 N. Staffs. moderate condition, evacuated 2/5 N. Staffs. condition fair, though stood empty. 2/6 N. Staff, moderate condition; 2 for debility. 3/5 S. Staffs condition fair a few thin ones. Evacuated 2 for debility; 2/6 Bde H.Q. 4 draught horses. In poor condition. 2 Coy A.S.C. Condition good;	
"	19/10/17		2/2 2/3 Condition very good. The Brigade is without staff entire. No clipping yet done in 2/6 N + 2/5 N.	
"	20/10/17.		Inspection with O.C. Div Train 461 Field Coy. Condition fair. About 6 horses want poor receiving special treatment. Have no rugs yet. 469 Coy Condition fair, without rugs.	
"	21-10-17		Visited M.V.S. Inspected all horses 59th Div Signals. Condition very good.	

WAR DIARY or INTELLIGENCE SUMMARY.

(Erase heading not required.)

Instructions regarding War Diaries and Intelligence Summaries are contained in F.S. Regs., Part II. and the Staff Manual respectively. Title pages will be prepared in manuscript.

D.A.D.V.S.

Army Form C. 2118.

Place	Date	Hour	Summary of Events and Information	Remarks and references to Appendices
CHATEAU de la HAIE	22-10-17		Visited M.V.S. Some fifty cases are being evacuated on 23rd inst. from Railhead at BARLIN. Arranged with S.H.Q. for 12 men to be permanently attached to Section for work on unloading & unloading etc. Inspected with O.C. Div Train 144 Bde H.Q. & Army Veins. Condition good, 3rd Section condition good, 4th Section good. The Fold Amb very moderate, The Fold Amb very moderate, are getting boiled feed.	
"	23-10-17		Visited proposed new location of M.V.S. at Ablain St NAZAIRE. It is unsuitable as no water nearer than 300 yards. Visited B/295 Bde yref A.V.S. & Coys. There are 20 cases of Pulma fever in this Battery & in B/296. Arranged for adoption of method to check spread of infection. Inspected all animals A/296: condition poor, 10 animals evacuated for debility. Visited 10th Bde, with A.D.V.S. & Corps. to investigate outbreak of billous fever. Number of cases at present in 296 Bde. A 9. B 22. C 5. D 3.	
"	24-10-17		Inspected all horses A/295 Bde. The condition of horses generally is poor & there is evidently need of better horse management. Debility cases for evacuation in this unit. Inspected C/295 animal: much better than the previous Battery: 3 cases of debility for evacuation. Inspected A/296: arrival in fair condition. They are without shelter or rugs & are very exposed position.	
"	25-10-17		Proceeded to proposed new location of M.V.S. at BARLIN. Reconnection for new horse Section. There is a horse dip near by. It is proposed to leave a collecting Section at PETIT SERVINS where units will continue to have their evacuation horses. Attended a board of examination of horses south at 152 Heavy Bty R.G.A.	
"	26-10-17		Attended Conference of A.D.V.S. & Corps. Inspected all animals C/295, about 20 very thin animals remainders in moderate condition.	
"	27-10-17		In view of the fact that C/purgosties Lymphangitis has occurred in the Rt Division Visited 295, 296 Bdes. & Inspected their sick animals weeding 40's of mange. of course of overhauling conference this disease with Celulitis.	
"	28-10-17		Visited Vety Detachment of 144 Y. T. & 152 My Bty. Got to take steps to deal with an outbreak of mange. Proceeded to Corps. to consult A.D.V.S. Proceeded to Mobile Laboratory at BARLIN to make some Bacteriological examinations.	
"	29-10-17		Visited Vety Detachment of 2/J.A. whose animals have improved since previous inspection. Inspected with O.C. Train the following units Y & 8 Sherwood, No. 1 Coy A.S.C., 3rd F.A., 144 & 147 M.G. Coys, 3rd J.A. have markedly improved during week as also 1st Sherwood.	
"	30-10-17		The 6 Men units were good.	
"	31-10-17		Inspected all animals of 1st Kent Heavy Bty & Corps. Cast 3 for Vety reasons. Visited detachment of M.T.Z.	

W.E. Bright

Major A.V.C.
D.A.D.V.S. 59 Div V.

(A7693). Wt. W12839/M1293. 75,000. 1/17. D. D. & L., Ltd. Forms/C.2118/14.

WAR DIARY or INTELLIGENCE SUMMARY

Army Form C. 2118.
D.A.D.V.S. (N.H.) DIVISION.

D.A.D.V.S. November 1917

Place	Date	Hour	Summary of Events and Information	Remarks and references to Appendices
CHATEAU de la HAIE	Nov 1.		Visited 2/1 Field Ambulance, R.E. Dump Coy, M.V.S. Barlin, Ox & Bucks L.I. Coufigny, 1st Can A.S. Coy Coufigny, 1st Toulaire Park A.D. HERSIN.	
"	2nd		Visited 295 & 296 Bde R.F.A. & 118 Inf Bde.	
"	3rd		Attended conference of ADVS I Corps. Visited 2/3 Field Amb. at SOUCHEZ.	
"	4th		Visited 145 M.G. Coy. Inspected at Horse B295 Bde. Here were some 26 markedly thin ones of which 5 were evacuated for debility. The condition of remainder was very insufficient. No system of giving any especial treatment to this one which were weathered throughout the battery. Reported the condition to R.S.P.A. asking that a capable wagon line officer be posted to the Battery. These matters given attention to.	
"	5th		Inspected all horses Divl Signal & M.M.P.	
"	6th		A.D.V.S. & Remount I Corps made preliminary inspection of animals proposed for casting for Remount Reserve. Nominated Veterinary cases.	
"	7th		Examined all animals C/295 Bde & M.T. Sect S.A.C. Condition of animals in both units fairly good.	
"	8th		A.D.V.S. I Army inspected animals for casting for Remount Reserve. Several animals were rejected as being serviceable for other purposes. It was evident that O.C's responsible for putting the animals forward for casting were in some cases quite unacquainted with the capacity or high grade of horse, or the animal which were rejected would not have come forward.	
"	9th		Visited 118 Bde & 476 Field Coy. Visited Artillery Brigade to inspect their surplus side with view to selecting some suitable for M.M.P. Only one suitable.	
"	10th		Attended a conference at A.D.V.S. I Corps. Received instructions to send a detachment from M.V.S. to help the Corps Mobile Detachment at DROVIN. Pointed out the disability under which the M.V.S. would labour in having to supply the detachment & another at the Collecting Station at Barlin besides sending parties to Base with evacuations. The orders redrawn were now withdrawn. Visited M.V.S.	
"	11th		Visited 476 Field Coy, 178 Inf Bde. 145 M.G. Coy. evacuated 5 chronic cases to M.V.S.	
"	13th		Visited all units 118 Bde 476 Field Coy & 143 M.G. Coy with reference to clipping. Saw some animals in 8 Sher Dn which had been clipped in the early part of October. These animals had now quite a good second coat. Sufficient to serve as a good protection through winter. Visited 4th Reserve Park at OLHAIN. Inspected horses. D.R.V.S. I Army at O.V.S. Nozhn came to A.H.Q. to investigate the case of Glanders evacuated by this M.V.S. from 79 R.F.A. Bde. The case occurred in Estaples outside his Divisional area.	

WAR DIARY
or
INTELLIGENCE SUMMARY

(Erase heading not required.)

Army Form C. 2118.
E.A.D.V.S.,
(N.Z.) DIVISION.

Place	Date	Hour	Summary of Events and Information	Remarks and references to Appendices
CHATEAU de la HAIE	15th		Visited M.V.S. at BARLIN. 1st Canadian M.V.S. arrived at BARLIN & is taking over location of this Divisional M.V.S.	
"	16th		Inspected all horses B/295 Bde. Have improved somewhat during the past week but there is today on a good deal of improvement. The grooming is indifferent, many horses are unfed with lice nits at the foot of the tail. I advised CRA to clip all legs in addition to belly over the buttocks proof of this tail.	
"	17th		Inspected all horses 4/295 Bde. The horses have improved since last inspection & are now in moderate condition but require more grooming. Total No. of both Batteries I cond. 4 slightly blind in one or both eyes. I totally blind in one eye.	
HERMAVILLE	18th		Moved with Division to HERMAVILLE.	
BASSEUX	19th		Moved with Division to BASSEUX. M.V.S. at BASSEUX.	
"	20th		Require orders from DDVS that in the event of the Division moving I will remain here until further orders. Asked QA.Q.M.G. to be allowed to bivouac as there is nothing to occupy our new & alternatively I be allowed to attach myself temporarily to a Casualty Clearing Station where my services may be of use. Am told to remain at REBREUVE.	
"	21st		At BASSEUX with M.V.S. Visited Division at ACHIET le PETIT.	
"	22.		Visited Division at ACHIET le PETIT. Asked O.C. Div. Train to further experiment with the metal plates in connection of picked up nails with Nos. 2 & 4 Coys Train. Detailed V.O. Train to take over Vety. Charge of all units in the Division as far as possible.	
"	23		M.V.S. moved to ACHIET le PETIT. Wrote to ADVS & Corps acquainting him that I am unable to render any returns reps 22.a. I am entirely out of touch with the Division & that only one V.O. is at present with the Division & that it will be impossible for him to carry on Vety. Charge of the whole Division efficiently.	
"	24		At BASSEUX. Visited VI Corps. Headquarters. Saw Major BLAIREVILLE reference evacuation of a horse left in his charge by D.A.C. I am still endeavouring to return according to return but am totally out of touch with Division. Am not acquainted with its location at BASSEUX.	
ETRICOURT	26		Moved to ETRICOURT to join Division.	
"	27		Visited IV Corps. C.C.S. (Veterinary) spects. A.D.V.S. Corps. O.C. M.V.S. posted 1 NCO & 1 men to the CCS for duty with evacuations. Visited the units.	
"	28.		(A 5050) Wt. W. 1235d/M. 3595. 73,000. 10/17. D. D & L., Ltd. Forms/C. 2118/24. 446 Field Coy. + 4/5 M.G. Corps.	

**D.A.D.V.S.,
59th
(N.M.) DIVISION.**

No. ....
Date ....

Army Form C. 2118.

WAR DIARY
or
INTELLIGENCE SUMMARY.

(Erase heading not required.)

Instructions regarding War Diaries and Intelligence Summaries are contained in F. S. Regs., Part II. and the Staff Manual respectively. Title pages will be prepared in manuscript.

Place	Date	Hour	Summary of Events and Information	Remarks and references to Appendices
	29.4.		Visited lines of 1/6 1/4/4 Bdes. Inspected horses of 19th Reserve Park & arranged for Veterinary Supervision.	
	30.4.		M.V.S. at Ericourt. In view of the fact that Guard Division M.V.S. remains at Metz, it is unnecessary to move this M.V.S. forward yet. Arranged with Guard Div M.V.S. to take our Casualties.	

15.V.17 G.M.
Major A.V.C.

Army Form C. 2118.

D.A.D.V.S.
8th
(M.L.) DIVISION.

WAR DIARY
or
INTELLIGENCE SUMMARY.
(Erase heading not required.)

December 1914

Instructions regarding War Diaries and Intelligence Summaries are contained in F. S. Regs., Part II. and the Staff Manual respectively. Title pages will be prepared in manuscript.

Place	Date	Hour	Summary of Events and Information	Remarks and references to Appendices
VALLULART WOOD	1st		D.H.Q. moved to VALLULART WOOD P.32 b.5.5. M.V.S. at ETRICOURT where it is too far from first line transport to be of any service. It is intended to move M.V.S. to METZ on vacation of site there by Guards Divisional M.V.S. The location of first line transport is around RIBECOURT & at A.9.d.4.6. Rode out to find a suitable location for M.V.S. as METZ is unsuitable on account of heavy shelling. Found dugouts & a small clearing in wood alongside road at P.27.C.4.4. & suitable clearing for advanced Aid Post at A.15.a.5.4. in vicinity of 178 Bde Transport.	
	2nd		M.V.S. & Advanced Aid Post moved to the location chosen. Visited both also wagon line of 174 Bde & 2/2 Field Ambulance.	
	3rd		Visited wagon lines of 178 Bde. Field Coys & Aid Post.	
LITTLEWOOD	4th 5th		D.H.Q. moved to LITTLEWOOD Camp. P.26.B.2.2. Units commenced to draw full hay ration. I noticed the very large concentration of transport & open horse lines without cover & protection around the Crow Road at P.17.& 6.7. & drew the attention of the A.D.V.S. V Corps to the matter in view of the danger from bombing raids. Visited M.V.S. & Advanced Aid Post. Arranged with Q.M. to issue expermental iron plates for the prevention of picked up nails to all Field Ambulance, all Train Companies & all Infantry Battalions, and the following numbers of ADs in each unit to be shod with them. Field Ambulance each 20 horses. Train Coys each 12 horses. Infantry Battalion each 9 horses.	
	6th		The experiment is to be carried out under Transport & Veterinary Officers supervision & reports forwarded in due course. During the week ending 6th inst there have been 21 casualties from bombs, 160 from shell. There were mostly due to transport being too far forward. Of the above numbers 40 animals were killed, or at mortality of 20% of the Division for the week.	
	7th		Attended a Conference of A.D.V.S. V Corps. Visited M.V.S. & Advanced Aid Post.	
	8th		Inspected all animals of D.H.Q. & M.M.V.S. Visited M.V.S. & Casualty Clearing Station & asked A.D.V.S. Corps that the 1 N.C.O. & P men attached to the latter for conducting duties may be withdrawn.	
	9th		Rode out to 295 & 296 Bdes at HAPLINCOURT. Found 5 cases of stomatitis in A Bty 296 Bde. Saw that due precaution were taken to prevent spread of the disease & reported matter to A.D.V.S. Artillery animals are receiving an extra 2 lb of oats for the next 14 days.	
	10th		Inspected 178 Bde wagon line in HAVRINCOURT WOOD. Sent a party to HAPLINCOURT WOOD to disinfest the troughs twenty been used by our Artillery	
	11th			

(A7092). Wt. W12859/M1293. 75,000. 1/17. D. D. & L., Ltd. Forms/C.2118.14.

Army Form C. 2118.

D.A.D.V.S.
59th
(N.M.) DIVISION.

WAR DIARY
or
INTELLIGENCE SUMMARY.
(Erase heading not required.)

December 1914

Instructions regarding War Diaries and Intelligence Summaries are contained in F. S. Regs., Part II. and the Staff Manual respectively. Title pages will be prepared in manuscript.

Place	Date	Hour	Summary of Events and Information	Remarks and references to Appendices
LITTLEWOOD	12th		106 Brigade of Artillery moved their waggon lines to VALLULART WOOD. Inspected for Stomatitis every animal in the infected Battery, & arranged isolation & separate watering for their cases. The 2/5 N.Staff moved their waggon lines into a field at NEUVILLE recently occupied by Stomatitis cases, against the advice of Capt Cook, A.V.C. I reported the matter to A.D.V.S. ordered their removal. Segregation separate watering. 148 Bde Transport have had 19 casualties including 2 killed in their present location from Shell during the past six days. I asked H.Q. that they be brought further back.	
" "	13th		Inspected all the animals of the Advanced sections of Artillery Brigade at METZ for Stomatitis. Visited W.Y.S. waggon lines of 178 Bde.	
" "	14th		The casualties from Shell during the past week were 18 killed or 9% of the Divisional Strength. The number of cases of Stomatitis in A Battery 296 Bde has increased to 9. It is considered the disease is well in hand & that a majority of animals are immune from the previous year. I reported to A.D.V.S. Corps that there is absolute lack of attempt to protect animals against bomb in this area. I sat a warning put in S.R.O. by the Division W.Y.S. has evacuated 150 cases to Casualty Clearing Station during the past week.	
YPRES.	15th 16th		Moved my office to P20 & 4.3. Attended a conference of A.D.V.S & Corps. Took over administration from D.A.DVS 47 Divn of 135 & 236 Bde, R.F.A. 140 Infantry Bde. & several other of his units arranged for removal & BUS of 47th Divn W.Y.S. for it to act as a Stomatitis Section.	
" "	17th		W.Y.S. moved into NEUVILLE. It is a very suitable location vacated by London Divl W.Y.S. Visited 296 Bde. Wagon Lines at RUYAULCOURT, examined the Stomatitis cases. I arranged a separate watering point for the whole of 2/296 Bde. By the Canal Bank. Inspected the animals of 2/3 Field Ambulance. Their condition has improved & is now good.	
" "	18th		Visited 295 Bde at BERTINCOURT and W.Y.S. also W.Y.F. 47th Divn at Bus. They have 80 care of Stomatitis under treatment from 47th Division.	
" "	19th		Inspected 174 Bde. with O.C. Divl Train. The general condition has fallen very considerably. 2/4 Lincoln. Poor & Shoeing bad & little grooming. Ale H.Q. animals dirty & Shoeing neglected. 2/4 Leicester condition fair. Grooming bad & Shoeing very neglected. 2/5 Lincoln. & the breeding 2/5 Leicester much the best. I reported these matters to D.H.Q. Also saw 144 M.G.Coy their animals were in good condition.	
" "	20th		Visited 296 Bde & M.Y.S.	

(A7092). Wt. W12859/M1293 75,000. 1/17. D. D. & L., Ltd. Forms/C.2118.14.

Army Form C. 2118.

D.A.D.V.S.,
59th (N.M.) DIVISION.

WAR DIARY
or
INTELLIGENCE SUMMARY.
(Erase heading not required.)

December 1914.

Instructions regarding War Diaries and Intelligence Summaries are contained in F. S. Regs., Part II. and the Staff Manual respectively. Title pages will be prepared in manuscript.

Place	Date	Hour	Summary of Events and Information	Remarks and references to Appendices
YTRES.	21st		The number of cases of Stomatitis has increased to 11 in A/296 Bde, but the outbreak has been confined to this Battery. Inspected 19th Reserve Park & 6 Bn Canadian Railway Troops.	
"	22nd		Attended a conference of A.D.V.S. V Corps. Inspected 174 Bde wagon lines at NEUVILLE & M.V.S. moved to LE CAUROY.	
LE CAUROY.	23rd		All transport moved by road to ACHIET-LE-PETIT. M.V.S. moved to ACHIET-LE-PETIT. Found billets for M.V.S. in LECAURDY.	
"	24th			
"	25th		All transport moved to area around LE CAUROY. Roads in very bad condition & horse lies great difficulty in getting along. M.V.S. moved to LE CAUROY.	
"	26th		Visited units in 176 Bde area — practically all animals under cover.	
"	27th		" " 174 Bde area.	
"	28th		" " 178 Bde area.	
"	29th		Roads again very bad owing to beaten snow & ice. The condition of animals generally has suffered a good deal during the past week owing to the state of roads, the extreme cold, the long distance supplies have to be fetched from the refilling points & the severe exertion during the march into the present area when some units were out for 16 hours on end on ice covered roads.	
"	30th		Inspected A/B H.Q. & M.V. lines Ingrael. The experimental iron plate for the prevention of picked up nail laws has been in use sufficiently long enough to form an opinion on their utility. The conclusion come to is that they are hardly stout enough. The frog depression become flattened down on & the frog after a few days use casting considerable frog pressure. The sample plate is hardly large enough for the large footed H.D. horses. When horse shod with these we compelled to work on hard ground & hot on roads, under the condition of the past fortnight, i.e. frozen ground the plate quickly	
"	31st		Visited 295 & 296 Bde & D.A.B. & examined some animals for evacuation for debility. The outbreak of Stomatitis is now at an end.	

W.E. Upton 7.4.
Major A.V.C.
D.A.D.V.S. 59 Divn.

Army Form C. 2118.

**D.A.D.V.S.,
59th
(N.M.) DIVISION.**

WAR DIARY or INTELLIGENCE SUMMARY.
(Erase heading not required.)

January 1918.

Instructions regarding War Diaries and Intelligence Summaries are contained in F. S. Regs., Part II. and the Staff Manual respectively. Title pages will be prepared in manuscript.

Place	Date	Hour	Summary of Events and Information	Remarks and references to Appendices
LE CAUROY	1-1-18		Visited 467 Field Coy R.E. "24 " 2/3 Field Ambulance to inspect animals with view to casting "6" in results of experimental plate for prevention of picked up nail.	
"	2-1-18		Visited Divisional Artillery.	
"	3-1-18		Major Bright D.A.D.V.S. proceeded on leave. Capt. Sooby visited 1/F. Bde H.Q. & 476 Field Coy.	
"	4-1-18		Inspected with O.C. Div. Train 1st Line Transport 178 Bde. Condition fair.	
"	5-1-18		" " " " " " 176 Bde. 2/5, 2/6, & 2/4 Sherwood. Condition fair. 2/5 N Staff; Condition fair; Shoeing good. 2/5 S Staff; Condition fair, shoeing good. Instructed officer i/c of 2/5 S Staff to feed 4 times daily not sets to be put on line after horse have finished their 4th feed (boiled).	
"	6-1-18		Inspected with O.C. Div. Train 1st line Transport 2/6 S Staff. Condition "Shoeing good. 3 or 4 poor ones getting extra feeds 2/6 N Staff. Condition marked improvement since last inspection.	
"	7-1-18		Visited FREVENT with horse of 2/8 Sherwood. Inspected 476 Field Coy R.E.	
"	8-1-18		Inspected with O.C. Div. Train 1st Line Transport of 2/8 Sherwood. Inspected 470 Field Coy R.E. 2/2 Field Ambulance.	
"	9-1-18		Inspected horse of No 3 Coy A.S.C. 144 M.G. Coy & first line transport of 1/4 Inf. Bde.	
"	10-1-18		Inspected with C.O.B. 2/6 South & 2/6 North Staff. Visited 2/5 Sherwood & 178 Bde. H.Q.	
"	11-1-18		M.V.S.	
"	12-1-18		M.V.S.	
"	13-1-18		Inspected 2/6 & 2/4 Sherwood.	
"	14-1-18		Visited FREVENT for entraining of sick animal.	
"	15-1-18		M.V.S.	
"	16-1-18		Inspected horses 467 Field Coy. Visited 175 M.G. Coy 2/2 Field Amb. & 470 Field Coy.	
"	17-1-18		M.V.S.	
"	18-1-18		Visited 296 Bde. R.F.A. to inspect horse of Battery Commanders to be replaced. 476 Field Coy. Major Bright returned from leave.	
"	19-1-18		Inspected animals of D.H.Q., M.M.P. & Signals.	
"	20-1-18		Rode to FREVENT to see the loading of evacuations. Some 30 animals mostly debility case from Artillery. Inspected all horse 3rd Field Amb.: Condition good. Most animals require standing on hoof & gravelled. 144 M.G. Coy Mules in good condition. All animal require training on feet most on quarters. 3 Coy Train Condition Shoeing good. But case of stomatitis recovering. Many animals require standing on Quarters. 1st Field Amb Animal & shoeing good. Animal require standing on feet.	
"	21-1-18			
"	22-1-18			

D.A.D.V.S.,
59th (N.M.) DIVISION.

Army Form C. 2118.

No 2

WAR DIARY
or
INTELLIGENCE SUMMARY.
(Erase heading not required.)

Place	Date	Hour	Summary of Events and Information	Remarks and references to Appendices
LE CAUROY	22.1.18		Quartier 469 Field Coy: Condition leaves a good deal to be desired. Coats all very hard. Inspected all horses of D Battery 295 Bde at IVERGNY. C Battery fairly good condition though somewhat uneven. Some 15 then over. Many animals require trailing in quartir. The standings are at the side of the road on the road itself as the field are impossible after the rain. Shoeing good. The unit has no field forge & asked me if I could assist them, but in view of G.R.O. 3149 I am unable to.	
	23.1.18		D Battery. Condition fairly good. About 10 this over requiring special attention. Shoeing good. One scheme banding of V on Quarter required. I have arranged that in this & 296 Bde. all cases of debility be sent to Battery sick lines, but under charge of the A.V.C. Sergt of the Battery. Inspected M.V.S. Arranged for improving their standings which are in a very bad condition. Saw D.A.D.V.S. at WARLIN in reference to various matters including the exclusive No of shoes drawn by some units. Took over Capt Lodby's duties on his going on leave.	
	24.1.18		Morning at M.V.S. Arranged with O.R.E. to effect improvements to standings of M.V.S. which are very bad & insanitary. Visited 148 Bde Group. Capt Lodby proceeded on leave.	
	25.1.18		Inspected all horses "A" "B" Batteries 295 Bde. A/295: Horses in a very fair condition but lack grooming. Shoeing good. B/295: This Battery has improved as regards condition a great deal during the past 3 weeks. 4 horses are now in good condition. All horses in the Brigade are now in standings made by the tradesmen & any little more anything that would be a feature in the field of the village which are nice deep in mud mostly, after the recent snows. Inspected tech side of all units. Very good equipment. Afternoon: Rode round 148 Bde Group & attended their sick.	
	26.1.18		At M.V.S. all day inspecting equipment & store of the Section.	
	27.1.18		Inspected D.H.Q. horses. M.V.S. Visited Corps H.Q. to discuss measures to be taken against scabies. Lee & other questions.	
	28.1.18		Rode to LUCHEUX, inspected all animals of B Battery 296 Bde. This Battery is the best in the 2 Brigades. So far as their horse management goes. Animals were in good condition grooming better than the Batteries. Afternoon: went with O.C. Divnl Tram to 2/1 Field Ambulance at BUNEVILLE to arrange for certain changes in the personnel of their Transport. Visited 148 Bde H.Q. on return. The cat ration is reduced by 2 lbs for all animal from this date.	

No 3

Army Form C. 2118.

D.A.D.V.S.,
59th
(N.M.) DIVISION.

WAR DIARY
or
INTELLIGENCE SUMMARY.
(Erase heading not required.)

Instructions regarding War Diaries and Intelligence Summaries are contained in F. S. Regs., Part II. and the Staff Manual respectively. Title pages will be prepared in manuscript.

Place	Date	Hour	Summary of Events and Information	Remarks and references to Appendices
LE CAUROY	29.1.18		Rode to LUCHEUX & inspected all animals of 296 Bde R.F.A. This Battery is as regards the condition of its horses by far the worst of the two Brigades of Artillery. Called the attention of the C.R.A. to the state of affairs making suggestions for their improvement. Reference the sand of 560 lb of Linseed to the Division for the month of February, this is being issued to M.V.S who in its turn will issue 380 lb to Artillery (i.e. 45 lb per Battery) & 180 lb to Infantry. At M.V.S. for evening stables.	
	30.1.18		Visited 295 Bde at IVERGNY to see the progress of treatment of some lice cases. I find the simplest remedial measure for lice is combing with a fine steel comb the teeth of which are so close as to arrest both lice & nits. This is preferable to any kind of washing & infinitely cheaper in the long run. Visited M.V.S & continued inspection of their equipment.	
	31.1.18		Visited 296 Bde at LUCHEUX. Inspected all horses of A & C Batteries. A Battery. The condition & grooming are fair as also the shoeing. Evacuated 2 cases of Debility & 2 of Ophthalmia. C Battery. Condition fairly good, & better than A's & B Batteries. Grooming & shoeing also fairly good. 5 Sore backs from using a surcingle without a roller. Attended M.V.S.	

W. Wright
Major A.V.C.
D.A.D.V.S.
59 Division

Army Form C. 2118.

WAR DIARY
or
INTELLIGENCE SUMMARY.
(Erase heading not required.)

D.A.D.V.S.
59th (N.M.) DIVISION.

February 1918.

Place	Date	Hour	Summary of Events and Information	Remarks and references to Appendices
LE CAUROY	Feb 1st		Visited 2/2 Field Ambulance at BUNEVILLE & gave a lecture to the NCOs i/c of Transport on Horse Management, Care of their animals, & explained the lines on which wastage could be avoided in forage, gear & casualties.	
	2nd		Saw all sick in 178 Bde area visiting the various units. Visited with O.C. Train & inspected animals of 178 Bde. a very marked improvement in the Horse management is shown since the inspection of 19.12.17. when a very adverse report was sent to H.Q. Division.	
			Brigade H.Q. Condition & grooming good. One H.D. evacuated for Ophthalmia	
			4th Lincolns. Condition generally good, though room for improvement. Since 4 this animals receiving special food & care.	
			4th Leicester. Condition, shoeing & grooming good. One horse evacuated for debility and old age.	
			5th Lincolns. Very good in every respect.	
			5th Leicester. Condition fair & shoeing neglected. Warned Transport officer that I would inspect again within a week when the shoeing must be satisfactory.	
			Inspected No 3 Coy Divisional Train. Attended M.X.S.	

WAR DIARY or INTELLIGENCE SUMMARY

Army Form C. 2118.

D.A.D.V.S.,
59th (C.M.) DIVISION. No 2.

Place	Date	Hour	Summary of Events and Information	Remarks and references to Appendices
LE CAUROY	Feb 3rd		Inspected animals of B.H.Q. & M.M.P. & Signals. Routine duties at M.V.S.	
	4th		Rode to FREVENT to supervise entraining of 21 cases for evacuation to Base. To 178 Bde H.Q. at HOUVIN on routine duties. Routine duties at M.V.S.	
	5th		To 296 Bde. R.F.A. to inspect some animals. Recommended for casting. Visited D/296 Bde to see what improvement is taking place in the Horse management after my complaint to C.R.A. on the subject on the 29th ult. Routine duties at M.V.S. in afternoon.	
	6th		Visited & inspected the following units. 1/4 M.G. Coy. PERNIN. Condition satisfactory. Pointed out to Transport Officer the wastage of forage in the Unit due to not using hay nets. 2/5 Leicester L'IGNEREUIL. Condition good. 2/4 Leicester L'IGNEREUIL. 2 Ride horses have been clipped but during last few days contrary to G.R.O. Reported to O.C. Brigade, as also re wastage of forage. 2/5 S/Staff MANIN. Horses very uneven & in many cases a neglect of grooming and general care. Showing bad Old Transport Officer. Would see again in a week. Wrote T.O.i/c asking why this neglect had not been reported to me. 200 M.G. Coy. PERNIN. Condition satisfactory. Wastage of forage going on in this Unit. Pointed out to Transport Officer.	

WAR DIARY or **INTELLIGENCE SUMMARY.**

(Erase heading not required.)

Army Form C. 2118.

D.A.D.V.S. 59th (2/M.) DIVISION.

Place	Date	Hour	Summary of Events and Information	Remarks and references to Appendices
LE CAUROY	6/1		2/1 Sherwood Foresters MAGNICOURT. Condition satisfactory. Artillery moved into New Area.	
"		7h.	Routine duties at M.V.S. & Office	
"		8h.	Routine duties at M.V.S. & Office. Capt. G.E. Grobey A.V.C. returned from leave. Capt H.W. Davies A.V.C. proceeded on leave. 176 & 178 Bdes left for new area. M.V.S. evacuated 11 horses from FREVENT.	
"		9h.	M.V.S. left for MONCHIET under instructions from 147. who moved to GOUY-EN-ARTOIS. en route for new area. Routine duties in office & examination of various scrapings for mange from Divl Artillery.	
GOMIECOURT	10h.		Rode from LE CAUROY to new area. GOMIECOURT. M.V.S. moved to ERVILLERS. At BEHAGNIES. Was not found. Wagon lines of 295 Bde R.F.A. with Staff Captain R.A. We called attention of Officers to the great wastage of forage equipment & material evident from which the outgoing units were responsible. The wastage was very considerable. I saw in the line of the Brigade at the point where they had been in the habit of using feeds, enough small hay, seeds etc & corn to feed about a hundred animals. I picked up rugs, blankets out of the mud, portions of harness, leather work, formidable rope, uniform etc etc. Arrangements were made for the salvage parties of the Batteries to collect all such materials. The grooming of the animals is quite insufficient & C.R.A. promised to make a point of this to C.R.A. asked that at least two periods of 15 x 1 hr daily be insisted on.	

WAR DIARY
or
INTELLIGENCE SUMMARY.
(Erase heading not required.)

Army Form C. 2118.

D.A.D.V.S.,
59th
(N.M.) DIVISION.

No 14

Instructions regarding War Diaries and Intelligence Summaries are contained in F. S. Regs., Part II. and the Staff Manual respectively. Title pages will be prepared in manuscript.

Place	Date	Hour	Summary of Events and Information	Remarks and references to Appendices
GOMIECOURT	11th		Inspected with C.R.A. All wagon lines 295 Bde (BEHAGNIES) and 296 Bde (HAMELIN COURT). 9 cases of mange in D/296 Bde. Arranged re Sulphide washing & disinfecting of animals, gear & standing of this Battery. Inspected M.V.S. at ERVILLERS. The standings are in ruined barns & sheds & there is accommodation for about 60 animals. There is good accommodation for men & plenty of material to effect improvements.	
MORY	12th		Moved my office to L'ABBAYE DUMP. MORY. Visited 295 Bde wagon lines & M.V.S. Visited D.H.Q. Arranged with D.A.Q.M.G. as to course to be followed in dealing with outbreak of mange in 296 Bde. Visited M.V.S. & D Battery 296 Bde.	
"	13th		It was arranged to handwash all animals of the 2 affected Batteries on 3 successive occasions with Sulphide, disinfecting Stables & all gear each time.	
"	14th		Visited D.H.Q. Visited M.V.S. & inspected cases for evacuation on 15th. Inspected animals of D.H.Q., M.M.P. & Signals. Inspected 469 Field Coy. in Company with C.R.E. The horse management is bad, condition & grooming bad & shoeing neglected. C.R.E. promised to take strong action in the matter.	
"	15th		Visited M.V.S. Visit of 2/2 Field Ambulance. The animals have gone off considerably in the past two months. Visited all units of 176 Bde and attended their sick.	

(A7093). Wt. W12839/M1293. 75,000. 1/17. D. D. & L., Ltd. Forms/C.2118/14.

Army Form C. 2118.

D.A.D.V.S.,
59th
(N.M.) DIVISION.

WAR DIARY
or
INTELLIGENCE SUMMARY.

(Erase heading not required.)

Instructions regarding War Diaries and Intelligence Summaries are contained in F.S. Regs., Part II. and the Staff Manual respectively. Title pages will be prepared in manuscript.

Place	Date	Hour	Summary of Events and Information	Remarks and references to Appendices
MORY	15th Oct		Visited 18th N.F. (Pioneers) at MORY & saw their sick. N.Y.S. evacuated from ACHIET LE PETIT.	
"	16th		Attended Conference of A.D.V.S. at Corps H.Q.	
"	17th		Visited M.V.S. There is accommodation in the location at ERVILLERS for following cases. Ophthalmia 17. Cellulitis 6. Skin 16. Debility 24. Surgical 14. They are improving standing billets. Visited 296 Bde. A. Battery, improving C. Battery, condition & grooming have gone back D. Battery, animals dirty & poor. B. Battery, fair. Saw the 6. R.A. in reference to D Battery & was assured an improvement would take place. Inspected lines & animals of the D.A.C.	
"	18th		The condition of animals is good, but there is no protection against bomb in some of the stables. Informed Q. of this. Visited Divl Train H.Q. The 4 Companies are accomodated at GOMIECOURT. Animals are in good standing with good bomb protection Visited & inspected the standing of D.A.C.	

Army Form C. 2118.

D.A.D.V.S.
59th
(N.M.) DIVISION

WAR DIARY
or
INTELLIGENCE SUMMARY.
(Erase heading not required.)

Instructions regarding War Diaries and Intelligence Summaries are contained in F.S. Regs., Part II and the Staff Manual respectively. Title pages will be prepared in manuscript.

Place	Date	Hour	Summary of Events and Information	Remarks and references to Appendices
MORY	19th		Accompanied D.D.V.S. Army & A.D.V.S. Corps on inspection of Artillery. The chief points to which D.D.V.S. drew attention were:—	
			1. Neglect in some cases on part of waggon line Officers to study the individual need of the few thin horses which were obviously not receiving the extra attention they should have.	
			2. Insufficiency of grooming	
			3. Inadequate provision of bomb protection in some cases & lack of uniformity of ideas as to the best methods of protection	
	20th		Arrived in the vicinity of an Advanced Vet. Post. at MORY. The Post consists of an evacuated cellar for new cattle & an open standing packed well round with earth & tree trunks for Post horses. Routine duties & microscopical examination of skin scrapings.	
	21st		Visited all units 176 Bde. Saw their sick & advised Transport Officers as to improvements which should be carried out to improve protection of stables against bomb. Inspected animals stables & advised against bomb. At D.H.Q. D.H.Q. M.M.P. Sul Signal & similarly advised. Visited 184 M.F. (horses) & inspected sick.	
	22nd		Visited 177 Bde units, inspected lines advising Transport Officers in reference to protection of stables against bombs. The failing is the omission to take into account the feature of the ground in the vicinity of the stables whether rising or falling & so to build protecting walls either too high or too low.	
	23rd		Attended Conference of A.D.V.S. Corps. Routine duties at office & microscopical examination of skin scrapings.	

Army Form C. 2118.

D.A.D.V.S.
59th
(2/M.) DIVISION

No 1

WAR DIARY
or
INTELLIGENCE SUMMARY.
(Erase heading not required.)

Place	Date	Hour	Summary of Events and Information	Remarks and references to Appendices
MORY.	24th		Inspected animals of S.H.Q. M.M.P. & Signals. There is insufficiency of Bomb protection in the stables of the latter & this was pointed out by me to O.C. Signals. Visited Railhead & inspected remounts coming for Division. Capt. R.W. Bance returned from leave.	
"	25th		Musketry Parade of M.V.S. Visited M.V.S. & inspected all animals for evacuation on the 26 inst. Visited lines of 178 Bde.	
"	26th		Visited 296 Bde. Inspected animals of D Battery & see progress of the measures for combating the mange outbreak. Visited M.V.S.	
"	27th		Good progress has been made in improvements to stables & standings & two dug-outs have been bunt up revetted for the men. Frequent dril parades for the men are being carried out & all equipment, rifles re inspected. Visited 295 Bde R.D.A. & saw some new animals proposed for evacuation. Musketry parade of M.V.S. at my office. Visited M.V.S. & B.Ho.	
"	28th		Dent Train & advised in reference to Bomb protection of the stables. Musketry parade of M.V.S. at my office. Visited M.V.S. & inspected all animals for evacuation on the 25th inst. Visited lines of 176 & 177 Bdes.	

Capt HowgH
Major A.V.C.
D.A.D.V.S.
59 Divn

59th Division

March 1918

Army Form C. 2118.

DADVS

WAR DIARY
or
INTELLIGENCE SUMMARY.

Date of arrival of unit in France:- 24th Feby 1917
Date of formation of Division:- 1st Nov 1914

Place	Date	Hour	Summary of Events and Information	Remarks and references to Appendices
BEHAGNIES.	1.3.18	—	Visited 296 Brigade R.F.A. and inspected animals in D. Battery for Mange. There have been no fresh suspects since 9th Feby. Sulphide washings commenced on 25th Feby. There is an improvement in the Horse Management of the Battery.	
	2.3.18		Musketry parade of M.V.S.	
	3.3.18		" " " Attended a Conference at office of A.D.V.S. V Corps. Inspected all animals of D.H.Q. M.M.P. & Signals. Shoeing of D.H.Q. is neglected. Measures for Foot Protection round the stables insufficient; reported these matters to Camp Commandant	
	4.3.18		Musketry parade of M.V.S. Visited & inspected the 3 Sections of D.A.C. Remounts for D Battery, 296 Brigade R.F.A. are being kept with H.Q. D.A.C. until the Battery is free from Mange. Visited Div¹ Train at GOMIECOURT.	
	5.3.18		Musketry parade of M.V.S. Asked for orders to be issued for measures to be taken in all units, at supply & R.E. dumps for the provision of boxes for reception of nails, in view of the somewhat large number of cases of pricked up nails occurring in the Division. Similarly at all forges & Q.M. Stores. Visited both Brigades R.F.A. to see progress of Ophthalmia cases & to advise as to the making of proper eyeshades consisting of simple blinkers with an edging of felt to cover forehead. Capt. R.C. Bickerton proceeded on leave.	
	6.3.18		Visited units of 177th Brigade groups; condition of all animals has considerably improved during the past	

59th Division

March 1918

Army Form C. 2118.

WAR DIARY
or
INTELLIGENCE SUMMARY.

(Erase heading not required.)

Place	Date	Hour	Summary of Events and Information	Remarks and references to Appendices
BEHAGNIES.	6.3.18		Some units have clipped out heels & back of pasterns & gave instructions that the practice must cease as the routine orders on the matter to quite definite.	
	7.3.18		Capt. J. Bradley took over temporary Veterinary charge of 295th Brigade R.F.A. & Capt. H.S. Dawes of D.A.C.	
	7.3.18		Visited M.V.S. inspected animals for evacuations & to see progress of Ophthalmia treatment. Atropine ointment as ordered by A.D.V.S. Corps for treatment of these cases is not available from base. Inspected animals of 3rd F.A. & found all horses in very good condition.	
	8.3.18		Conferred with D.v.C. Commander in reference to measures prescribing inquiries to reduce virulence of Ophthalmia. Visited 296th Brigade R.F.A. & inspected all horses in company with Horsemaster. D Battery was in process of carrying out the second Mange washing & there have been no fresh cases during past week. General condition of all animals improved. No signs of forage wasted. Arranged with Horsemaster to assist in procuring salvage material for resetting stables.	
	9.3.18		Attended Conference of A.D.V.S. V Corps. Visited M.V.S.	
	10.3.18		Inspected all animals D.H.Q., M.M.P. & Signals. Carried out microscopical examination of mange skin scrapings.	
	11.3.18		Inspected Brigade H.Q. 176th Brigade & remaining units of Brigade & attended Brigadiers Charger. Animals generally in very good condition. Inspected evacuations cases at M.V.S.	
	12.3.18		Visited 295th Brigade R.F.A. Inspected sick lines & Veterinary equipment of all four Batteries.	

59th Division

March 1918

WAR DIARY
or
INTELLIGENCE SUMMARY.
(Erase heading not required.)

Army Form C. 2118.

Place	Date	Hour	Summary of Events and Information	Remarks and references to Appendices
BEHAGNIES	13.3.18		Visited 296th Brigade R.F.A. Inspected sick lines & Veterinary equipment of all four Batteries.	
	14.3.18		Visited various units in Division to inspect all recent Remounts. Saw evacuation cases at M.V.S.	
	15.3.16		Visited 296th Brigade R.F.A. Saw sulphide washing of D Battery horses & disinfection of stables &c. This completes the 3rd washing since 25th Feb, since when only one suspect has been found.	
	16.3.18		Attended conference of A.D.V.S. V Corps	
	17.3.18		Inspected all animals D.H.Q., M.M.P. & Signals.	
	18.3.18		Visited 176th Brigade Group.	
	19.3.18		" " 177th " "	
	20.3.18		Inspected all first line transport with A.D.V.S. Corps 178th Brigade. Conditions good. 177th Brigade: Condition good. 2/4th Lincolns: not quite up to standard. 178th Brigade: Condition very good. All three Field Ambulances & 467th Field Coy very good. A.D.V.S. Corps expressed himself as satisfied with the general condition of the animals.	
	21.3.18		Moved my office to BEHAGNIES. German attacks commenced, owing to heavy shelling of back areas first line transport moved back to COURCELLES LE COMTE as also did M.V.S. Divisional artillery passed into Administration of 40th Division. Capt. R.C.Bickerton returned from leave.	

59th Division

March 1918

Army Form C. 2118.

WAR DIARY
or
INTELLIGENCE SUMMARY.
(Erase heading not required.)

Place	Date	Hour	Summary of Events and Information	Remarks and references to Appendices
BUCQUOY	22.3.18		Moved my office to BUCQUOY. M.V.S. moved to AYETTE.	
BOUZINCOURT	23.3.18		Moved by route march to BOUZINCOURT with first line Transport & M.V.S. A 12 mile march in hot sun but animals stood journey well.	
	24.3.18		At BOUZINCOURT.	
CONTAY	25.3.18		Left at 2 a.m with all first line transport & M.V.S. for CONTAY. March about 7 miles.	
FIENVILLERS	26.3.18		Left at 6 a.m with all first line transport & M.V.S. for FIENVILLERS - CANDAS area. March about 15 miles under good conditions.	
	27.3.18		-	
VILLERS CHATEL	28.3.18		Proceeded by road via DOULLENS, FREVANT, ST POL, LE LAPUGNOIR thence to Villers Chatel & MINGOVAL, first line transport & M.V.S. proceeded by route march to HERLIN LE SEC area, a 20 mile march.	
MINGOVAL	29.3.18		M.V.S. marched to MINGOVAL. First line transport marched to CAUCOURT-HORDAIN area, about 15 miles.	
"	30.3.18		-	
"	31.3.18		First line transport & M.V.S. moved to LILLERS, a 16 mile march. Animals are suffering somewhat from the inclement weather of the past few days & the lack of shelter in the various Camps in many cases billets for horses have been unobtainable.	

6.F.Bright
Major A.V.C
59th D.V.A. Surgeon

DUPLICATE
Original

59th Division.

April 1918.

Army Form C. 2118.

WAR DIARY
or
INTELLIGENCE SUMMARY.

(Erase heading not required.)

Place	Date	Hour	Summary of Events and Information	Remarks and references to Appendices
COUTHOVE	1.4.18		Moved by road from MINGOVAL to COUTHOVE near PROVEN. 1st Line transport moved to MORBECQUE & marched about 15 miles. M.V.S. also to MORBECQUE area.	
"	2.4.18		At Chateau COUTHOVE. M.V.S. moved to WATOU, PROVEN area & 1st line transport moved to COUTHOVE. marched about 12 miles.	
"	3.4.18		Visited Headquarters of D.A.D.V.S. 33rd Division to discuss the taking over of his M.V.S. at BRANDHOEK. Visited Corps Headquarters to report to A.D.V.S. VIII Corps to discuss Veterinary arrangements in this Corps. There is a Veterinary Evacuating Station at P.18.d.9.4. (Sheet 28) to which animals may be sent in batches of not less than 8 on any day. 6 men are to be permanently detached from M.V.S. to the Veterinary Evacuation Station for conducting duties.	
"	5.4.18		Visited site for M.V.S. occupied by 33rd Division at Brandhoek to which this Divisional M.V.S. is moving on 7th inst. There is at present accommodation for 90 horses & 30 men & further accommodation for another 40-50 horses could be effected if necessary labour were forth-coming to repair standings. There is a great deal of work required in the camp in the way of drainage & repairs. It is proposed to establish a rest camp here for about 40 debilitated animals & to provide extra feeding. Saw D.A.D.V.S. 33rd Division in reference to taking over the area for Veterinary Administration. Visited M.V.S. & Divisional Train Headquarters, G, A. & Q. Staffs moved to advanced Headquarters at YPRES.	

59th Division
April 1918

2

Army Form C. 2118.

WAR DIARY
or
INTELLIGENCE SUMMARY.
(Erase heading not required.)

Place	Date	Hour	Summary of Events and Information	Remarks and references to Appendices
GOUTHOVE	4.4.18		Visited units of 147 Brigade Group & inspected animals & standings. This Brigade has stood the recent marching better than the other two & has fewer thin horses. Visited 2/1 (N.M.) M.V.S.	
"	6.4.18		Attended conference of A.D.V.S. VIII Corps. Sent in a report to Division to complain as to the very adverse conditions under which animals of 5th North & 6th South Staffs are standing, their standings in open fields without shelter & asked that stabling be found for them.	
Brandhoek	7.4.18		Moved my office to H.Q. A. 94 (Sheet 28). 2/1 (N.M.) M.V.S. moved to BRANDHOEK. Visited lines of S.A.A. section D.A.C. in stables with good standings. Brigade Headquarters 176th Brigade & the 3 Battalions. 176th Brigade & N. Staffs are in very bad muddy open standings without shelter but have not suffered from the hardships of the past fortnight. 2/6th S. Staffs are also in bad muddy standings without shelter but have suffered a good deal & are not looking well. 2/6 N. Staffs are in stables & looking well. C. Coy M.G. Coy are also in open standings in mud.	
BRANDHOEK	8.4.18		As the Divisional Transport is at the moment stretched out over an area over 20 miles in length. I to take Veterinary Charge temporarily rearranged Veterinary charge. I to take Veterinary charge of units in POTIEJE - YPRES area, Capt Sooby to take charge of units in BRANDHOEK area & Capt Dawes with Headquarters at WATOU to take charge of units in WATOU - WINNIZEELE area.	
"	9.4.18		Inspected all 3 Field Coys, 468th boy has improved considerably during the past month. Saw C.R.E. animals, M.G. Battalion & H.Q. Coys & D. Coys M.G. Battalion & b/4 Royal Scots Fusiliers.	

59th Division

WAR DIARY
or
INTELLIGENCE SUMMARY.
(Erase heading not required.)

April 1918

Army Form C. 2118.

Place	Date	Hour	Summary of Events and Information	Remarks and references to Appendices
BRANDHOEK	30.4.18		Visited 174/176 Brigade Lines at BRANDHOEK. Visited 2/1(N.M.) M.V.S.	
"	1.4.18		Visited Field Companies, 59th Machine Gun Battalion & 6/7th Royal Scots Fusiliers.	
"	2.4.18		Moved my office to ABEELE. 2/1(NM) M.V.S. moved to ABEELE, L.31.C.64.	
"	3.4.18		Visited 176th Brigade Transport & Divisional Train Headquarters.	
BOESCHEPE	14.4.18		Moved my office from ABEELE to BOESCHEPE. Divisional Transport moved to RENINGHELST-WESTOUTRE, LOCRE area. 2/1 (NM) M.V.S. remained at ABEELE.	
"	15.4.18		Visited Divisional first line transport, Divisional Train & 2/1(NM) M.V.S. (ABEELE). As there are 3 M.V.S.'s within easy distance of our transport, it is not considered necessary to move up our M.V.S. Received visit from A.D.V.S. IX Corps. All evacuations are via V.E.S. at WIPPENHOEK.	
"	16.4.18		Visited units in the WESTOUTRE area. Visited M.V.S.	
"	17.4.18		Division suffered heavy casualties owing to hostile shelling, having 20 horses & 1 mule destroyed. The losses occurred mostly among the heavy draft-horses of Divisional Train.	
"	18.4.18		Visited M.V.S. & advanced Divisional headquarters.	
COUTHOVE CHATEAU	19.4.18		Moved my office to CHATEAU, COUTHOVE. 2/1(NM) moved to ST. SIXTE. Came into VIII Corps Administration.	
	28.4.18		At CHATEAU COUTHOVE. Brigade Transports moved into VLAMERTINGHE west area.	
VOGELTJE	29.4.18		Moved my office to VOGELTJE. M.V.S. moved to BAMBECQUE with 1st Line Transport & Divisional Train.	

59th Division.

April 1918.

Army Form C. 2118.

WAR DIARY
or
INTELLIGENCE SUMMARY.
(Erase heading not required.)

Instructions regarding War Diaries and Intelligence Summaries are contained in F. S. Regs., Part II. and the Staff Manual respectively. Title pages will be prepared in manuscript.

Place	Date	Hour	Summary of Events and Information	Remarks and references to Appendices
VOGELTJE	22-4-18		At VOGELTJE. The Brigade areas are some 12 miles from Divisional Headquarters.	
"	23-4-18		Visited transport lines of 177th & 178th Brigade Groups at HOUTKERQUE.	
"	24-4-18		Visited Corps Headquarters at CASSEL to discuss various matters with A.D.V.S. Corps. Evacuations are by V.E.S. at WIPPENHOEK & PROVEN.	
BAMBECQUE	25-4-18		Moved my office to BAMBECQUE. Visited 178th Brigade area & No. 3 Divisional Train. Took over temporary charge of M.V.S. during the illness of Capt. G. G. Scotty.	
VOGELTJE	26-4-18		Visited 177th Brigade area. Routine duties at M.V.S. Brigade moved out of resting area for operations. Moved my office to F.22.d. (Convent) Sheet 27. M.V.S. remained at BAMBECQUE.	
"	27-4-18		Visited 73rd Field Ambulance to see a suspected rabid dog. Visited 176th Brigade Transport Lines.	
"	28-4-18		Attended at No. 4 Coy Divisional Train as President of a Board of Examination on Shoeing Smiths of 178th Infantry Brigade.	
"	29-4-18		Arranged to continue the Board on Shoeing Smiths, but owing to the moving back of 177th & 178th Brigades Transports to HOUTKERQUE, this had to be postponed.	
"	30-4-18		Visited 6/7th Royal Scots Fusiliers. Inspected animals for cooking at 2/2nd Field Ambulance.	

6FVA-1948. Major. A.V.C.

D.A.D.V.S. 59th Division.

WAR DIARY or INTELLIGENCE SUMMARY

Army Form C. 2118.

59th (N.M.) DIVISION.

Place	Date	Hour	Summary of Events and Information	Remarks and references to Appendices
VOGELTIE	1.5.18		Attended a Board of shoeing South at 176th Infantry Brigade at HOUTKERQUE. 5 men qualified.	
"	2.5.18		Inspected Stafford Brigade Transport Lines. Inspected 59 M.B. Battalion Headquarters R.A.P. Companies.	
"			D Coy mules were not in good condition & require better supervision, grooming &c.	
"	3.5.18		Attended Board on Shoeing visits of 176 Brigade & by R.S.L.Watkins at D.H.Q. transport lines.	
"			Made inspections of A.V.C. Companies M.G. Battalion. The mules of the Coys/Companies are in good condition &	
"			condition of Animals satisfactory. The shoeing of the Battalion is unsatisfactory. The transport	
"			Officer promised to remedy these points	
"	4.5.18		Visited 176th Brigade Group	
"	5.5.18		Inspected animals of D.H.Q. Signal Coy & M.M.P.	
"	6.5.18		Move by road to ST. OMER.	
ST. OMER	7.5.18		Visited Veterinary Hospital ST. OMER. M.V.S. moved to RUBRUCH.	
"	8.5.18		M.V.S. moved to ST. OMER. Rode to ST. MOMELIN to meet M.V.S. Untanged killed by M.V.S. in Veterinary Hospital at ST. OMER.	
"	9.5.18		M.V.S. moved to BLESSY.	
"	10.5.18		Moved by road from ST. OMER to E.P.S. Saw 1 Line Transport on road. M.V.S. moved to PRESSY-LES-PERNES.	
E.P.S.	11.5.18		At E.P.S.	
"	12.5.18		M.V.S. moved to E.P.S. Interviews D.M.S.Y A.M.B. & Divisional Cavaly. Visited A.D.V.S. X Corps to discuss Veterinary arrangements in this area.	

WAR DIARY or INTELLIGENCE SUMMARY

Army Form C. 2118.

D.A.D.V.S.,
59th (N.M.) DIVISION.
No. 76967
Date 7.6.17

Place	Date	Hour	Summary of Events and Information	Remarks and references to Appendices
E.P.S.	13/5/17		Visited 176 Brigade Transport at NEDON, thence to 177 Brigade Transport at TOURS. In view of large number of units not under administration of the Division & the large extent of the area, I obtained services of another V.O. Capt. D.S.P.m.o. A.V.C. who will take charge of 176 Brigade group & another Vet. Officer. of M.V.S. will attend Central Group. 178 & 179 we attached & V/S. Divisional from the Southern Group. (174 Brigade & attached units)	
"	15/5/17		Inspected 74 Field Ambulance at NEDON CHELLES; they are short of 7/6 remounts. Some of these are old which I strongly recommended them to graze. Army as much as possible. Visited C.A. Section D.A.C. The mules are in very moderate condition & very backward in their coats. Deficient of remounts. Capt. McDavid A.V.C. proceeded on return from charge of 6th Battalion from 20th to ETAPLES.	
"	16/5/17		Inspected 177 Brigade units. 2/3 Lowland Ambulance; 73 Lett Ambulance; fair, & some 12 poor H. animals, & improved in the road for grazing. 2/8 Lowland A. Condition very good. 5th Essex Condition very good. We inspect Staithes 176 Somerset L.I. S.A. bad Condition; these are vicious animal what I am returning to go mounts. I am certain L.I. in very good Condition. 174 Brigade H.Q. very good; evacuated 2 lame horses. The new units complain generally as to lack of field forges most of them are short of Curtabb shoes, which is a rate of 3 or 4 per day. There is a lack of hoof protection of stable standings. I am taking the matter up through headquarters	

WAR DIARY or INTELLIGENCE SUMMARY

Army Form C. 2118.

Place	Date	Hour	Summary of Events and Information	Remarks and references to Appendices
E.P.S.	17/5/18		Inspected 176 Brigade Units. 2/1 Field Ambulance. Condition fair & about 10 British animals improved over them the need for grazing as much as possible. Mr R.C. Fusiliers animals in good condition & horses in such an appalling state that the unit is hardly fit to take the road. Arranged to loan them animals & forage from D.A.C. for a few days to take the matter in hand. 73 Field Ambulance Animals in poorish condition with exception of 4 Flemish cows which are being grazed. M.V.S. move d. to DIEVAL.	
"	18/5/18		Visited S.A.A. section D.A.C. & 176 & Coy Divisional Train.	
"	19/5/18		Inspected all animals H.Q. Signal Coys M.M.P. Visited A.D.V.S. at Corps Headquarters. Capt. Matthews o. A.V.C. returned from accompanying transport to base.	
"	20/5/18		Visited detachment 2 A.T. Auxiliary Horse transport at FIEFS, & 178th Brigade Training Camp. Capt. M.N.L. Burley A.V.C. moved to N°3 Coy 59th Divisional Train.	
"	21/5/18		Visited 175 K AT Coy at FREDEFIN.	
"	22/5/18		Visited 177th Brigade Training & Lieut. G. Potter K.R.R.	
"	23/5/18		Visited S.A.A. section D.A.C. N°4 Coy Divisional Train & Divisional Signals.	
"	24/5/18		Visited Corps Headquarters.	
"	25/5/18		Visited N°1 Coy Divisional Train Animals in good condition. Visited S.A.A. section D.A.C. Having generally looking as they should & considerably improved. Visited Headquarters as to the condition of this unit and	

WAR DIARY
or
INTELLIGENCE SUMMARY.
(Erase heading not required.)

Army Form C. 2118.

D.A.D.V.S.
39th (N.Z.) DIVISION.
No. 7698 T.
Date 7.6.18

Instructions regarding War Diaries and Intelligence Summaries are contained in F. S. Regs., Part II. and the Staff Manual respectively. Title pages will be prepared in manuscript.

Place	Date	Hour	Summary of Events and Information	Remarks and references to Appendices
E.P.S.	28.5.18		cont. with that an endeavour be made to improve them. Visited Corps Headquarters to discuss Veterinary arrangements with A.D.V.S. Corps.	
"	29.5.18		Inspected animals of D.H.Q. & Signals.	
"	30.5.18		Visited 176th Brigade Group with D.A.A.G. 11th R.S.F., 34th & the animals are now that is in the morning. 2nd R.I.R. Condition fair. Lots of shoes will be cast yet ready before the Farriers of leave to rejoin D.A.C. 33rd Stephine? & guide more strain of cicab backwards. Standings in new field & no cover protection. Condition fair. Shoeing backwards many feet in broken condition through continual during wet backwards to the gun treatment required.	
"	29.5.18		Visited 177th Brigade Group Units.	
"	31.5.18		Visited 116th Brigade Headquarters with D.A. & Q.M.G. & A.D.V.S. Corps. It was a storm got in regard to the unsatisfactory state of horse management prevailing among the Garrison Battalions of the Brigade, that Corps Horse master should be posted to Brigade Headquarters for a short while to instruct the Transport personnel in the matter. He inspected 16.0.2 Coy Divisional Train, including the animals of 66th Divisional Train recently attached, the latter were in fair Condition & are improving rapidly.	

W.F. Wright. Major A.V.C.
D.A.D.V.S. 39th Division

D.A.D.V.S., 59th

Army Form C.2118

No. ~y/81.V.
Date 1.7.18

WAR DIARY
or
INTELLIGENCE SUMMARY
(Erase heading not required.)

59th (N.M) Division.

Place	Date	Hour	Summary of Events and Information	Remarks and references to Appendices
EPS.	1.6.18		Routine duties in office.	
"	2.6.18		Visited 176 Brigade group units. 11th G. Bn. Lancashire – So far condition & improving, require more grooming. #31 Field Coy R.E. condition had some 15 thin ones. I asked the C.O. to see what remedial improvement were made. 1/5th G. Bn. Royal Sussex – condition fair. 1/4th G. Bn. Royal Welch Fusiliers – condition indifferent but improving rapidly. Showing backwards too much clipping. 2/3rd G. Bn. Lancashire Fusiliers – So far condition.	
"	3.6.18		Visited WAVRANS, & inspected animals of 1/2nd (N.M) Field Ambulance.	
"	4.6.18		Routine duties at D.H.Q. Rode to LUGY to inspect animals in Charge of Area Commandant there.	
"	5.6.18		Visited units in 177 Brigade Group. 2/5th G. Bn. K.R.R., Condition of animals fair & improving. 76 Durham L.I. Animals fair in condition & making very slow improvement. Showing be[?]... This unit has made excellent progress in making tent protection around horses from use of ... but the work has been stopped by Brigade owing to alleged damage to the fields in which the animals are. I am reporting matter to the Division as the actual damage only represents about a tenth the value of the most indifferent animal they have on the transport of this Battalion. Routine duties in office.	
"	6.6.18		Inspected D.H.Q. Signals & M.M.P. There have been a few cases of colic among the post with farm...	

D.A.D.V.S.
Army Form C2118.
(N.M.) DIVISION.
No. M/81/V
Date 1.7.18

59th (NN) Division

WAR DIARY
or
INTELLIGENCE SUMMARY.
(Erase heading not required.)

Place	Date	Hour	Summary of Events and Information	Remarks and references to Appendices
E.P.S.	7.6.18		Inspected 1/2nd Field Ambulance, Headquarters N° 2 Coys of 12th Army Auxiliary Horse Transport.	
"	8.6.18		S.A.A. Section D.A.C., Train. Detachments 1st Army Auxiliary Horse Transport at FIEFS & LIGNY; 1st Coy 59th Divisional Train.	
"	9.6.18		Visited 12th Army Auxiliary Horse Transport, D.H.Q. & Divisional Signals.	
"	10.6.18		Visited 176 Infantry Brigade Area & 1st Coy Divisional Train.	
"			Visited 2/1 (NN) M.V.S. & met A.D.V.S. X Corps there. Accompanied O/C M.V.S. to K. Southwestern Premier roundsman pit condition, showing very neglected. Arranged to examine Forges showing Smith 4th Siege Coys R.W.R.E. Arranged to transfer O'Keaney (Forge of this unit to H.Q. Divison on account of the distance from its present V.O. 11 miles. 2/3 Field Ambulance. The numerable knee fallen off considerably during the past 2 weeks owing probably to this having lost their Warrant Officer. Called attention of O.C. Divisional Train to the matter asking of the feeling of another suitable N.C.O. could be expedited.	
"	11.6.18		Visited Divisional Signal Coys, D.H.Q. & 12th Army Auxiliary Horse Transport.	
"	12.6.18		Visited 2/1 Field Ambulance, 1/7th G Bn Royal Sussex & 1/7th G Bn Worcester Regt; Condition of Cattle not improving.	
"	16.6.18		Visited S.A.A. Section D.A.C., D.H.Q. & Signals.	

D.A.D.V.S.,
59th
(N.M.) Division.

Army 3

WAR DIARY
or
INTELLIGENCE SUMMARY.
(Erase heading not required.)

59th (N.M.) Division

Place	Date	Hour	Summary of Events and Information	Remarks and references to Appendices
EPS.	19.6.18		Visited D.H.Q. to inspect horses of D.H.Q. & Divisional Signals. Visited 1st Army Laundries	
			Transfer of charge of attached units belonging to 1st Army troops on leaving HESTRUS area.	
	20.6.18		Moved my office to BONY.	
	21.6.18		M.V.S. moved to Bony. Capt Cooky A.V.C. took over D.A.D.V.S. duties from Major Bright who	
			proceeded on leave to U.K.	
BONY.	29.6.18		Visited 20th & 1st Bn Liverpool Regt, 4th & 5th Bn Royal Welch Fusiliers, 17th & Bn Royal Sussex Regt	
			Hoy Inspection Trains 11th Bn Royal Scots Fusiliers & Headquarters Divisional Train	
	20.6.18		Visited D.H.Q. Signals A.M.P. & 71 Field Ambulance.	
	21.6.18		Visited 2 Coys Divisional Train & general inspection duties.	
	22.6.18		Visited 20th & Bn Liverpool Regt, 4th & 5th Bn Royal Welch Fusiliers & Headquarters Divisional Train	
	23.6.18		Attended G.O.C. inspection of M.V.S.	
	24.6.18		Visited D.H.Q. & M.M.P. & general routine duties in office.	
	25.6.18		Inspected with J.C.O. Divisional Train 1st line transports, No. 6 Brigade Headquarters, 14th & Bn	
			Royal Sussex Regt, 4th & 5th Bn Royal Welch Fusiliers, 20th & Bn Liverpool Regt, 11th & Bn Royal Scots	
			Fusiliers, 20th & Bn Kings Rifle Corps, 16th & Bn Durham Light Infantry & 71 Field Ambulance.	

D.A.D.V.S.,
59th
(N.M.) DIVISION.
Form C.2118.
Date 1.7.18

Army 4

59th (N.M.) Division.

WAR DIARY
or
INTELLIGENCE SUMMARY.
(Erase heading not required.)

Instructions regarding War Diaries and Intelligence Summaries are contained in F. S. Regs., Part II. and the Staff Manual respectively. Title pages will be prepared in manuscript.

Place	Date	Hour	Summary of Events and Information	Remarks and references to Appendices
Bony	26.6.18		Visits M.M.P. L° & Coy Divisional Train & Signal Coys.	
"	27.6.18		Inspected with o/c Divisional Train, 197th Infantry Brigade Headquarters, 11th G. Bn Somerset Light Infantry, 13th G. Bn Essex Regt, & 7/2 Field Ambulance.	
"	28.6.18		General office routine.	
"	29.6.18		Inspected 11th G. Bn Royal Scots Fusiliers, 7/6th G. Bn Durham Light Infantry, 10th G. Bn Essex Regt, 11th G. Bn Somerset Light Infantry, 2.5 G. Bn Liverpool Regt, & 36th G. Bn Northumberland Fusiliers.	
"	30.6.18		General routine duties.	

Ruy J. Loeb
Capt A.V.C.
for Major D.A.D.V.S. 59th Division

D.A.D.V.S.
59th
(N.M.) DIVISION.
Army Form C. 2118.

59th (N.M) Division.

WAR DIARY
or
INTELLIGENCE SUMMARY.
(Erase heading not required.)

July 1918

Vol 18

Place	Date	Hour	Summary of Events and Information	Remarks and references to Appendices
BOMY.	1.7.18		Inspected with O/C 59th Divisional Train, 36 Northumberland Fusiliers, 178 Infantry Brigade HQ 2/6 Sherwood Foresters T.C., 13 West Riding, 2/3 (N.N) Field Ambulance, & S.A.A. Section, D.A.C.	
"	2.7.18		Visited 2/5 Liverpool, 4 Royal Welch Fusiliers, 11 Royal Scots Fusiliers, Heavy Divisional Train, 1/5 Royal Sussex, & 176 Infantry Brigade H.Q.	
"	4.7.18		Major Bright, D.A.D.V.S. returned from leave.	
"	5.7.18		Office duties. Visited 2/1 (N.N) M.V.S.	
"	6.7.18		Visited 176 Infantry Brigade Group, 2/1 (N.N) Field Ambulance, & inspected standings of lines.	
"	7.7.18		Inspected animals of D.H.Q., Signal Coy & M.M.P. Condition good.	
"	8.7.18		Visited 177 Infantry Brigade Group & inspected lines, also 7/2 (N.N) Field Ambulance.	
"	9.7.18		Visited 178 Infantry Brigade Group & 7/3 (N.N) Field Ambulance, & inspected horse lines & standings.	
"	10.7.18		Visited S.A.A. Section, D.A.C.	
"	11.7.18		Moved with D.H.Q. to MONCHY CAYEUX. 2/1 (N.M) M.V.S. moved to MONCHY CAYEUX.	
MONCHY CAYEUX	12.7.18		Visited 176 Infantry Brigade area to inspect horse lines & general arrangements.	
"	13.7.18		Inspected all animals D.H.Q., Divisional Signal Coy & M.M.P.	
"	14.7.18		Visited & inspected with Capt Dawes all animals S.A.A. Section D.A.C. This unit has improved very considerably in last month, & animals are now in good condition. Nº 3 Coy Divisional Train, animals in	

D.A.D.V.S.
59th
(N.M.) DIVISION.
Army Form C. 2118.
No. 740/V.V.
Date 4.8.18

59th (N.M.) Division

July 1918

WAR DIARY
or
INTELLIGENCE SUMMARY.
(Erase heading not required.)

Instructions regarding War Diaries and Intelligence Summaries are contained in F. S. Regs., Part II. and the Staff Manual respectively. Title pages will be prepared in manuscript.

Place	Date	Hour	Summary of Events and Information	Remarks and references to Appendices
MONCHY CAYEUX	14.7.18		in good condition with exception of 6 surplus ride horses & 2/2(N.M) Field Ambulance, animals very fair & about 12 animals unsatisfactory	
"	15.7.18		Visited & inspected with V.O. i/c all animals, following units 176 Infantry Brigade, 15 Essex Regiment. Condition of animals & general arrangements good. 2/6 Durham Light Infantry. Condition satisfactory, but shoeing backward. 11 Somerset Light Infantry. Conditions & shoeing good. Recommended Division to provide alternate standings, as the present lines are in a bad condition through rain.	
"	16.7.18		Office routine & M.V.S.	
"	17.7.18		Visited & inspected with V.O. i/c all animals 176 Infantry Brigade. Brigade H.Q. very moderate & require more attention from Staff Captain. Other units good. 2/1(N.M) Field Ambulance exceptionally so. 2/3 (N.M) Field Ambulance also very good.	
"	18.7.18		Visited in company with V.O. i/c & inspected all animals 178 Infantry Brigade - 13 West Riding, riders looking light, otherwise units good. Brigade H.Q. particularly good.	
"	19.7.18		Visited Divisional Train H.Q. & inspected all animals. Inspected all animals 2/2 (N.M) Field Ambulance which are still not altogether satisfactory.	
"	20.7.18		Visited 2/3 (N.M) Field Ambulance with Capt Dooby to judge in Transport Competition. The transport of	

D.A.D.V.S.
59th (N.M.) DIVISION.
No. 7407.V.
Date 4.8.18.
3

Army Form C. 2118.

59th (N.M.) Division

July 1918.

WAR DIARY
or
INTELLIGENCE SUMMARY.
(Erase heading not required.)

Instructions regarding War Diaries and Intelligence Summaries are contained in F.S. Regs., Part II. and the Staff Manual respectively. Title pages will be prepared in manuscript.

Place	Date	Hour	Summary of Events and Information	Remarks and references to Appendices
MONCHY-CAYEUX	20.7.18		of this unit is in very good condition now.	
"	21.7.18		Inspected all animals D.H.Q., M.M.P. & Divisional Signal Coy.	
"	22.7.18		Visited lines of 176 Infantry Brigade units to inspect standings & general arrangements, also 2/1 (N.M.) Field Ambulance.	
"	23.7.18		Visited 177 Infantry Brigade Group to inspect units & standings.	
"	24.7.18		Visited 178 Infantry Brigade Group & 2/3 (N.M.) Field Ambulance.	
"	25.7.18		Routine duties at office of M.V.S.	
"	26.7.18		Moved with D.H.Q. to BASSEUX. 2/1 (N.M.) M.V.S. moved to BASSEUX.	
BASSEUX	27.7.18		Inspected D.H.Q., 59 Signal Coys M.M.P. Visited lines of units in 176 Infantry Brigade Group.	
"	28.7.18		Inspected all animals 26 Machine Gun Battalion attached 59 Division. Condition fair generally & not so good as might be; the unit has some 20 recent remounts whose condition is improving. The standings of two companies are in a filthy state & I am endeavouring to get them either vacated or repaired.	
"	29.7.18		Visited 178 Infantry Brigade Group units & inspected lines & standings.	
"	30.7.18		Visited 177 Infantry Brigade Group & inspected lines & standings.	
"	31.7.18		Visited N°s 2,3,& 4 Coys Divisional Train & inspected lines & standings which are good. Visited	

D.A.D.V.S.,
59th
(N.M.) DIVISION.
Army Form C. 2118.
No. 7905/V
Date 4-8-18
H

59th (N.M.) Division.

July 1918.

WAR DIARY
or
INTELLIGENCE SUMMARY.
(Erase heading not required.)

Instructions regarding War Diaries and Intelligence Summaries are contained in F. S. Regs., Part II. and the Staff Manual respectively. Title pages will be prepared in manuscript.

Place	Date	Hour	Summary of Events and Information	Remarks and references to Appendices
BASSEUX	31.7.18		Visited 476 Field Coy R.E. & inspected all animals. This unit recently suffered 30 Casualties from bombs. The replacements are in fair condition & rapidly improving.	

W.F.Bright. Major.
D.A.D.V.S. 59th Division.

D.A.D.V.S.,
59th
(N.M.) DIVISION.
No. ......
Dated ....

Army Form C. 2118.

WAR DIARY
or
INTELLIGENCE SUMMARY.
(Erase heading not required.)

59th (N.M.) Division.

August 1918.

Instructions regarding War Diaries and Intelligence Summaries are contained in F.S. Regs., Part II. and the Staff Manual respectively. Title pages will be prepared in manuscript.

Place	Date	Hour	Summary of Events and Information	Remarks and references to Appendices
BASSEUX	1.8.18		Inspected 181 Brigade R.F.A. in company with V.O.:- B. Battery fair in condition & grooming fair; Headquarters Fair; A. Battery Fair; D. Battery Fair. Bomb protection insufficient & in need of repair; reported this to Divisional Artillery.	
"	2.8.18		Inspected all animals 470 Field Coy:- Condition good.	
"	3.8.18		Attended conference of A.D.V.S. VI Corps.	
"	4.8.18		Inspected all animals Dett. Q.M.G.P. & Divisional Signals.	
"	5.8.18		Inspected all animals 467 & 461 Field Coys:- The condition of latter is not up to standard of Division.	
"	6.8.18		O.K. Visited Corps Veterinary Evacuating station, Divisional Train Companies & 72 (NM) Field Ambulance - Latter unit is not up to general standard in condition-grooming which I reported to O.C.	
"	7.8.18		Inspected in company with V.O. i/c all horses 181 Brigade R.F.A. General condition of animals good, with exception of A. Battery which is only fair no regards condition & grooming.	
"	8.8.17		Visited 26 & Liverpools to choose horses for Divisional show. Visited D. Battery 181 Brigade R.F.A.	
"	9.8.18		Inspected in company with V.O. i/c all horses No 2 Division & D.A.C. condition of animals general horse management, extremely good.	
"	10.8.18		Inspected with V.O. i/c all horses No 1 Corps & Divisional Train. Visited 178 Infantry Brigade to select animals for Divisional Horse Show.	

D.A.D.V.S.
59th
(N.M.) DIVISION.
No. E.D.R.V.
Date 3.9.18

Army Form C. 2118.

59th (NM) Division

1st Aug 1918

WAR DIARY
or
INTELLIGENCE SUMMARY.
(Erase heading not required.)

Instructions regarding War Diaries and Intelligence Summaries are contained in F. S. Regs., Part II. and the Staff Manual respectively. Title pages will be prepared in manuscript.

Place	Date	Hour	Summary of Events and Information	Remarks and references to Appendices
BASSEUX	11.8.18		Inspected all horses D.H.Q. Signals & M.M.P.	
"	12.8.18		Attended Division Eliminating Competitions for Corps Horse Show.	
"	13.8.18		Inspected lines & Standings of 20th Batt. M.G.C. & reported adversely to Division.	
"	14.8.18		Visited 3/2(NM) Field Ambulance. Condition generally moderate & grooming insufficient. Reported conditions to O/C Divisional Train & F.M.S. Inspected Divisional Train Headquarters & horses under preparation for show.	
"	15.8.18		Visited 181 Brigade R.F.A. & in company with V.O. i/c visited all batteries to inspect sick.	
"	16.8.18		Visited 148 Brigade R.F.A. & inspected sick.	
"	17.8.18		Visited lines of all units 177 Infantry Brigade & inspected Standings & general arrangements.	
"	18.8.18		Visited lines of all units 178 Infantry Brigade. Attended conference A.D.V.S. Corps.	
"	19.8.18		Inspected with O/C Divisional Train all animals 72(NM) Field Ambulance, & 1st, 2nd, 3rd & 4th Corps Sick Train. Inspected lines of 21st M.G.C. at BAILLEULVAL-RIVIERE, to report as to their having carried out orders for improvement. Visited 179 Infantry Brigade at BARLY.	
"	20.8.18		Visited 178 Infantry Brigade units at BARLY.	
"	21.8.18		Visited 4(NM) Field Ambulance, advanced lines of 17th Infantry Brigade & 469 Field Coy R.E.	
"	22.8.18		Visited 176 Infantry Brigade Headquarters transport & Brigade units; 467 & 476 Field Coys R.E.	

D.A.D.V.S.,
59th
(M.M.) DIVISION.
Army Form C. 2118.

59th (N.M.) Division

Aug 1918

WAR DIARY
or
INTELLIGENCE SUMMARY.
(Erase heading not required.)

Instructions regarding War Diaries and Intelligence Summaries are contained in F. S. Regs., Part II. and the Staff Manual respectively. Title pages will be prepared in manuscript.

Place	Date	Hour	Summary of Events and Information	Remarks and references to Appendices
BASSEUX	23.8.18		Moved my office to BAYINCOURT. Divisional units moved to new area.	
BAYINCOURT	24.8.18		BAYINCOURT.	
"	25.8.18		Moves to NORRENT-FONTES. N.35. Sheet 36A.	
NORRENT FONTES	26.8.18		Visited D.A.D.V.S. VIIth Division at his Headquarters to discuss Veterinary arrangements in new area.	
"	27.8.18		Rode to TREIZENNES to inspect site for M.V.S.	
"	"		Moved my office to BUSNES. P.33. (Sheet 36A)	
BUSNES	28.8.18		M.V.S. moved to TREIZENNES. N.6 (Sheet 36A) Evacuations to Corps V.E.S. at GLOMENGHAM. O.24 (sheet 36A)	
"	"		Rode out to see units in new area.	
"	29.8.18		Visited Div. Train Companies of No.1 Coy to inspect latter which has been detached with artillery for past 6 months.	
"	30.8.18		Rode to GUARBECQUE, met O.M.V.S. & selected site for billets of M.V.S. Inspected 517th Royal Engineers - condition indifferent. Came to this area west of polish with equine evacuation. Animals have suffered a good deal from the long treks of previous week. Some units did 70 miles in two stays.	
"	31.8.18		Inspected animals of 11th S.L.I. 2/6th Scottish, 36th N.F., 7 & 7/6 Battns. - the latter are in indifferent condition & insufficiently groomed: there is lack of supervision. Inspected 418 & 470 Field Coy. Good, & 467 Field Coy. R.E., the latter very fair. Some 12 thin animals. There is an abundance of green fodder & grazing in the district, so Hay should be moved to GUARBECQUE. C.P. (sheet 36A).	

W F Lim? g Lt
A D V S 59th Division

59th (N.M.) Division

Sept 1918.

WAR DIARY
or
INTELLIGENCE SUMMARY.
(Erase heading not required.)

Place	Date	Hour	Summary of Events and Information	Remarks and references to Appendices
BUSNES	1.9.18		Inspected Animals of 2/6 K.W.E.N. R.S.E. & 2/6 K.R.R. Animals have generally benefited from good weather the last fortnight of the previous month.	
"	2.9.18		Rode to MOLENGHEM & inspected animals 432 Field Co R.E. Conditions sufficient, reported to A.D.V.S.	
"	3.9.18		Visited 2/(NM) M.V.S. Visited units of 69 Labour Group, with headquarters at BERGUETTE.	
"	4.9.18		Visited units 2/178 Infantry Brigade.	
"	5.9.18		Inspected units No 6 Infantry Brigade at ST FLORIS.	
"	6.9.18		Visited CALONNE to collect kit for M.V.S. Inspected cases 2/178 Infantry Brigade units.	
"	7.9.18		Visited 5 Batn B.W.I. Regt at TREIZENNE (N.6. S.E.36A.) 432 Field Co R.E. N. MACKENGHEM & (Q.16 S.E.36A.) & 64 Labour Group at O.1.C. (S.E.36A.) & Companies. Visited M.V.S & gave orders for move to Asylum ST VENANT. (Ry S.E.36A)	
ST VENANT	8.9.18		M.V.S moved to Asylum. Funny Q.19.a.6.0. (S.E.36A). Moved my office to Asylum ST VENANT (Ry S.E.36A.)	
"	9.9.18		Visited M.V.S. Visited 294. A.S. by at J.33. (S.E.36A)	
HAYSACK FARM.	10.9.18		Rent C.J. Leaky proceeded on leave to ENGLAND. Moved my office to Q.P.a.6.0. (S.E.36A)	
"	9.9.18		Visited 2/1 & 2/2 N.M. Field ambulances & inspected their animals	
"	10.9.18		Visited D.H.Q. Inspected Signals & M.M.P. Inspected animals of 2/176 Infantry Brigade units. They are mostly in the open in muddy fields. There being no shelter of accommodation. Animals have suffered during the past week from long journey	

D.A.D.V.S.
59th
(N.M.) DIVISION

Army Form C. 2118
No. ....
Date ..8..15./.9.......

59 (N.M) Division

Sept 1918

WAR DIARY
or
INTELLIGENCE SUMMARY.
(Erase heading not required.)

Instructions regarding War Diaries and Intelligence Summaries are contained in F. S. Regs., Part II. and the Staff Manual respectively. Title pages will be prepared in manuscript.

Place	Date	Hour	Summary of Events and Information	Remarks and references to Appendices
HAYSTACK FARM	10.9.18		Long journeys & amounts of work of vets. Visited 251. R.R. who are in a rest of Corps at Camp	
(J.4.d.6.8.)(36A)			at LA SOURGUE (J.33. SE 36A)	
"	11.9.18		At M.V.S. repairing info of buildings & standings. Executions to Capts Titney & counts of	
			station at GUARDECQUE P2.C.3.D.(36A)	
"	12.9.18		Visited A & B Batteries D/96 Brigade R.F.A & inspected animals with Capt Bradley A.V.C. Y.O/c	
			Horses looking well. B Battery have standings on canal bank path. Service of range of	
			water supply in canal should they get loose at night. Noted half broken R.E. b-	
			lacksmiths moved to adjacent hut which was one.	
"	13.9.18		Visited & inspected animals of C & D Batteries 96 Brigade R.F.A in company with V.O.	
			D/Battery, Animals looking well, as also C with exception of one section whose charge	
			is billeting made up to N.C.O. Y/c	
"	14.9.18		Visited M.V. Infantry Bde spare units & inspected standings & general arrangements.	
			Animals are recovering well from the recent strain, & there is now abundance of	
			grazing & loose in the neighbourhood of which they are taking full advantage.	
"	15.9.18		Visited 176 Infantry Brigade units & inspected general arrangements.	
"	16.9.18		Routine visits at M.V.C. In addition to repairs to buildings, the batten is labouring large	
			quantities	

DADVS.
596.
(N.M.) DIVISION
Army Form C. 2118.
No. ....
Date ....

59th (N.M.) Division

Sept 1918

WAR DIARY
or
INTELLIGENCE SUMMARY.
(Erase heading not required.)

Instructions regarding War Diaries and Intelligence Summaries are contained in F. S. Regs., Part II. and the Staff Manual respectively. Title pages will be prepared in manuscript.

Place	Date	Hour	Summary of Events and Information	Remarks and references to Appendices
HAYSTACK FARM	16-9-18		Quantities of material in the vicinity. In two days 950 complete 18 pounder shells & gas still cases have been gathered in from the fields.	
"	17.9.18		Visited Field Companies:- 469 Field Coy, animals were very moderate, arranged for C.R.E.6	
			Will talk with me at an early date.	
"	18.9.18		Visited various horse units in the neighbourhood, attached to me 1st Veterinary Charges was 25 A.T.R.K. & C.o. Poelcapelle R.E.	
"	19.9.18		Inspected all animals 2/5 K.R.R., 17 Royal Sussex, 2/ Norfolds 26 R.W.F.	
			2/5 K.R.R in good condition but require more grooming, some animals badly in need of shoeing.	
			7/2 Field ambulance, general marked improvement since last inspection. The three Battalions	
			are generally fair & should improve under present conditions	
"	20.9.18		Visited Train Corps A.S.C. & D.H.Q.	
"	21.9.18		Inspected with C.R.E. all animals 467, 469, 470 Field Coy.	
			Inspected all animals 174 Infantry Brigade, condition good generally.	
"	22.4.18		Inspected with O.C. Divisional train all animals Div. train, the general condition is very good.	
"	23.9.18		Inspected with A.A. & Q.M.G. all animals 178 Infantry Brigade units. Inspected all animals of Battn.	
			M.G.C. & Field ambulance. Condition of 178 Infantry Bde generally fair, & room for considerable improvement.	

D.A.D.V.S.
59th
Army (Form) ICVERSION.
No. S.2.2.V.
Date 21.3.18

59th (N.M) Division
Sept 1918

WAR DIARY
or
INTELLIGENCE SUMMARY.
(Erase heading not required.)

Instructions regarding War Diaries and Intelligence Summaries are contained in F. S. Regs., Part II. and the Staff Manual respectively. Title pages will be prepared in manuscript.

Place	Date	Hour	Summary of Events and Information	Remarks and references to Appendices
FARM. et	24.9.18		Moved my office to farm at R.M.a.q.q. (Sf.36A) & established Veterinary unit & Collecting Post there.	
R.M.a.q.q.(36.A)	25.9.18		Capt. C.G. Scoby A.N.C. returned from leave. Visited 295 Brigade R.F.A. & Batteries with V.O. i/c.	
"	26.9.18		Capt. H.S. Dawes A.V.C. proceeded on leave to ENGLAND. Visited 176 Infantry Brigade units.	
"	27.9.18		Visited 177 Infantry Brigade Units & 3/1 & 7/ Field ambulances.	
"	28.9.18		Visited 178 Infantry Brigade Units.	
"	29.9.18		Inspected animals of D.H.Q., M.M.P., & Div Signal Coy.	
"	30.9.17		Inspected with V.O. i/c animals of 295 Brigade R.F.A.. The condition is good and arrangements generally satisfactory except in C Battery where there are unusual number of injuries horses.	

L.F. Vor— 7 Lt Colonel
D.A.D.V.S. 59th Division

59th (N.M.) Division

October 1918.

Vol 22

WAR DIARY
or
INTELLIGENCE SUMMARY.
(Erase heading not required.)

Army Form C. 2118.

Place	Date	Hour	Summary of Events and Information	Remarks and references to Appendices
Farm Rue u.g.4.7 LESTREM.	1.10.18		D.D.V.S. V Army & A.D.V.S. XI Corps visited my office & inspected with me the following units:- B., C., D., Batteries 295 Brigade, C/296 Brigade R.F.A., D.D.V.S. expressed satisfaction at the general condition of animals.	
"	2.10.18		Visited units of 176 Infantry Brigade.	
"	3.10.18		Reconnoitred a location for M.V.S. in new Divisional front. Visited M.V.S. to arrange move.	
ESTAIRES. L22.c.6.6 (Sheet 36A)	4.10.18		My office & M.V.S. moved to L22.c.6.6 (Sheet 36A). 47th Divisional M.V.S. took over my Veterinary Collecting & aid post as a site for their M.V.S.	
"	5.10.18		Visited advanced I.H.Q. of 295 Brigade units & 476 Field Coy R.E.	
"	6.10.18		Reconnoitre site for M.V.S.	
"	7.10.18		Visited in company with V.O. 1/c, 2/5 K.R.R. & all Companies of 2nd Machine Gun Battalion. The animals of latter have just come from England & are of good type & in good condition. Transport officers generally are self contained with service conditions.	
"	8.10.18		Visited 1/5 Field ambulance. Condition satisfactory. Inspected animals of C.R.E. and 3 Field Companies. Reconnoitred advanced site for M.V.S. at BAC ST. MAUR.	
"	9.10.18		Inspected standings & general arrangements at 176 Infantry Brigade units.	
BAC ST MAUR.	10.10.18		Moved my office & M.V.S. to BAC ST MAUR. (G.17.c.5.5. 3F36). Visited advanced D.H.Q.	

Army Form C. 2118

WAR DIARY
or
INTELLIGENCE SUMMARY.
(Erase heading not required.)

59th (N.M.) Division.

October 1918.

Instructions regarding War Diaries and Intelligence Summaries are contained in F. S. Regs., Part II. and the Staff Manual respectively. Title pages will be prepared in manuscript.

Place	Date	Hour	Summary of Events and Information	Remarks and references to Appendices
BAC. ST. MAUR	1.10.18		Visited Companies of 200 Machine Gun Battalion in company with Battalion Transport Officer.	
"	2.10.18		Visited train companies in company with 59th Divisional Vet.n.	
"	3.10.18		Capt. H.E. Dawson returned from leave. Visited 176 Infantry Brigade train.	
"			Accompanied V.O. i/c in an inspection of 296 Brigade R.F.A. Animals generally are improving this condition & are taking full advantage of the young green forage available.	
"	4.10.18		Capt. G.C. Blackston proceeded on leave. (Accompanied V.O. i/c in an inspection of 295 Brigade R.F.A. Batteries good. well found.	
"	5.10.18		Inspected all animals I.H.B. Signals & M.M.P.	
"	6.10.18		Visited Divisional Companies & D.A.C.	
"	7.10.18		Division moved forward to Welsh Horse	
"	8.10.18		V.E.S. moved to LAVENTIE. Reconnoitered site for M.V.S.	
ST. ANDRÉ	9.10.18		Moved M.V.S. & my Office to ST. ANDRÉ (sheet 36). Left 3 animals in charge of 1 man at ST. ANDRÉ to work moving program of V.E.S. which moved to LAVENTIE; 1½ miles in rear.	/M.S.
HEM.	10.10.18		Moved my Office & M.V.C. to HEM (D.D. city. sheet) V.E.S. now about 3 miles in rear. Animals	
3.G.E.4.7.S??			of the division at the commencement of an advance from Divisional Area. As animals & enemy retreated & hostile shelling of S. ANDRÉ whilst unoccupied hence advising of the horses	

59th (N.M.) Division.

Army Form C. 2118.

WAR DIARY
or
INTELLIGENCE SUMMARY.
(Erase heading not required.)

October 1918.

Instructions regarding War Diaries and Intelligence Summaries are contained in F. S. Regs., Part II. and the Staff Manual respectively. Title pages will be prepared in manuscript.

Place	Date	Hour	Summary of Events and Information	Remarks and references to Appendices
H.E.M.	21.10.18		Evacuation are becoming increasingly difficult. It is hoped that in view of future advance V.E.S. will put forward an estimate cost between itself & the M.V.S. so that M.V.S. will not be overworked in the event of and till N.E.S. moves forward with the troops. Now discussing the matter with A.D.V.S. Corps at first opportunity.	
"	22.10.18		A.G. in Town with Q. Brigade have suffered somewhat lately, the past 10 days owing to the movement of the various Corps stages. They should soon recover as the weather does being so important, there is no absence of good ut.E.M. & Q. Brigade units.	
"	23.10.18		Visits to Infantry Brigade units. Visits V.E.S. LAVENTIE to look at their arrangements for evacuation.	
"	24.10.18		Visits 3 Field Coy R.E. & D.A.C.	
"	25.10.18		Inspected with O/C Divisional Train with convoy of Infantry Brigade; condition of 4 good. Sections have been greatly gaining up as above are working considerably on the last letter genereally only last about a fortnight.	
"	26.10.18		Inspected in company with O/C Div. Ammunition Column will animals of Infantry Brigade. The condition of the most hardships they have undergone was very satisfactory.	

59th (N.M) Division

October 1918.

Army Form C. 2118.

WAR DIARY
or
INTELLIGENCE SUMMARY.
(Erase heading not required.)

Place	Date	Hour	Summary of Events and Information	Remarks and references to Appendices
H.E.M.	29.10.18		Casualties all ranks of 6 Dragoon Guards Bridge. [illegible] are generally most ready number of horses are lower than establishment which they are unwilling to keep. They are short of Trough Reacting which is difficulty in getting back until the cavalry [illegible] of [illegible] were assured to arrange supply through our own D.A.V.C. Tickets e.g. of 6 Dragoon Guards has been out Divisional Artillery.	
	29.10.18		Shoots under taken by XI Corps Veterinary Hospital on our [illegible] as any unit of the [illegible] oxen is now under the care of 149 Infantry Brigade the walking wounded is very good + the ground not [illegible] arrangements convenient. [illegible] casualties of A+B own covering our Battalion	
	30.10.18		Visited Y+L Ambulance Supply field by R.E. Visited D.A.V.S. XI Corps.	
	31.10.18		Visited in company with C.D.V.S. XI Corps 1/4th Company R.A. + 9/40 Brigade R.A. The animals of both batteries did not appear to be both very satisfactory + good condition. The horses in [illegible] + ? aspects of 24 [illegible] Brigade battery the [illegible] seemed any most animals + stables were out of good symmetry. Report on same to copy forward to C.R.A.	

W.F. Knight Major
D.A.V.S.
59th Division

D.A.D.V.S.
59th
(N.M.) DIVISION.
Army Form C. 2118.

59th (N.M) Division

WAR DIARY
or
INTELLIGENCE SUMMARY.
(Erase heading not required.)

November 1918

Place	Date	Hour	Summary of Events and Information	Remarks and references to Appendices
SAILLY-LES-LANNOY.	1.11.18		Moved my office to SAILLY-LES-LANNOY (G.29.d.y.6. Sh.37). Visited 264 Travelling Veterinary Section in August. 28th A.T. Coy. & various labour units of XI Corps to arrange Veterinary administration in august. Two cases of suspected Rabies reported from forward area; arrived body of one dog & proceeded with it to PASTEUR Institute LILLE for examination, afterwards reported to A.D.M.S. stating that it would probably be impossible to give a definite diagnosis.	
"	2.11.18		Received a further report on another man bitten by a supposedly Rabid dog; took steps to obtain carcass, forwarded same to PASTEUR Institute. It is very unlikely that either this or the previous case were Rabies as no cases have occurred in the area where they were shot for several months. Visited 3/2 Field Ambulance.	
"	3.11.18		Inspected all animals D.H.Q. M.M.P. & Signal Coys. — Condition good all round.	
"	4.11.18		Inspected all animals Portuguese Artillery attached this Division. Art. Coy. Mules are generally infair to good condition whilst horses are generally poor & ill-nourished. The shoeing is in many cases very badly neglected & there is a shortage of shoes. Forage arrangements are not good & there is a certain amount of shortage. The units are now under the Divisional Administration & reported fully to Headquarters on them.	

D.A.D.V.S.
59th (N.M.) DIVISION
Army Form C. 2118.

WAR DIARY
or
INTELLIGENCE SUMMARY.
(Erase heading not required.)

59th (N.M) Division
November 1918

Instructions regarding War Diaries and Intelligence Summaries are contained in F. S. Regs., Part II. and the Staff Manual respectively. Title pages will be prepared in manuscript.

Place	Date	Hour	Summary of Events and Information	Remarks and references to Appendices
SAILLY-LES-LANNOY.	5.11.18		Received a report as to an suspected Rabid dog which had bitten a man of 2nd Machine Gun Battalion. As the dog was alive I went to TEMPLEUVE to see same & concluded the dog was not Rabid; reported to A.D.M.S.	
	6.11.18		Visited 296 Brigade & inspected wagon lines. Animals are improving generally in the present area.	
"	6.11.18		Visited D.A.C. sections. The animals are out in open & do not appear to be suffering from the somewhat inclement weather. Visited X1 Corps V.E.S.	
"	7.11.18		Visited Labour Group Units at HEM & WESQUEHAL & 284 A.T. Coy at latter.	
"			Visited Field Coys R.E.; Condition of animals of 467&470 Coys good & 469 Coy improving.	
"	8.11.18		Visited 176 Infantry Brigade Units. Animals doing well & showing improving.	
"			Visited & selected location for M.V.S. when Division moved forward.	
RAMEGNIES CHIN.	9.11.18		Moved my office to RAMEGNIES CHIN (J.5. Sheet TOURNAI) M.V.S. moved to BAILLEUL (J.4. TOURNAI)	
			Visited M.V.S.	
	10.11.18		Examined animals of D.H.Q., M.M.P., & Signal Coy. Route to FOREST (N.19.a. Sheet 57) to enquire into reported outbreak of Foot&Mouth Disease. In view of the practical absence of any animals in the area after the German evacuation no further steps were taken.	

D.A.D.V.S.,
59th
(N.M.) DIVISION.
Army Form C. 2118.

WAR DIARY
or
INTELLIGENCE SUMMARY.
(Erase heading not required.)

59th (N.M.) Division.

November 1918

Place	Date	Hour	Summary of Events and Information	Remarks and references to Appendices
RAMEGNIES-CHIN	10.11.18		Visited a German Horse Veterinary Hospital at METTES (J36.b&J37). The principle method of treatment adopted here appeared to be, (1) Application of tar-greasy dressing pads which the animal was put into a hot air chamber & sweated for 30 minutes. (2) Latterly gas treatment in brick chambers similar to those in use in our hospitals or sulphur Dioxide. The gas was let in from cylinders & the quantity measured by weighing the cylinder on a scale.	
"	11.11.18		Visited 2 g. Brigade R.F.A. & Brigade unit.	
"	12.11.18		Visited Train Coys. Visited 176 Infantry Brigade unit & 7/6 (N.M.) Field Ambulance.	
"	13.11.18		Visited 177 Infantry Brigade Units & Machine Gun Battalion.	
"	14.11.18		Visited 246 Brigade R.F.A. & inspected standings. Animals are maintaining condition.	
"	15.11.18		M.V.S. moved to TRESSIN'S (C.of) en route WATTIGNIES Area. Division en route to new area.	
WATTIGNIES	16.11.18		M.V.S. arrived at SECLIN (N.29.d.9.9. SH36). Moved my office to WATTIGNIES (N.1.C.6. SH36).	
"	17.11.18		Inspects D.H.Q. M.M.P. & Brigade.	
"	18.11.18		Visits M.V.S. Horses are accommodated in good stables whilst men are in infantry Evacuations are to LA MADELEINE, some 7 miles distant. Visited 290 Brigade R.F.A. Inspected A.B.C. Batteries. Animals are generally in excellent condition.	
"	19.11.18		Visited 2 g. Brigade R.F.A. & inspected B. & D Batteries.	

D.A.D.V.S.
53ᵃ
(N.M.) DIVISION.

Army Form C. 2118.

WAR DIARY
or
INTELLIGENCE SUMMARY.
(Erase heading not required.)

59th (N.M) Division.

November 1916.

Instructions regarding War Diaries and Intelligence Summaries are contained in F. S. Regs., Part II. and the Staff Manual respectively. Title pages will be prepared in manuscript.

Place	Date	Hour	Summary of Events and Information	Remarks and references to Appendices
WATTIGNIES.	20.11.16		Capt. J. Smithy V.O. i/c 296 Brigade R.F.A. proceeded on leave to England. Capt. R.C. Richardson took over temporary Veterinary Charge of 296 Brigade R.F.A.	
	21.11.16		Visited 296 Brigade R.F.A. Condition generally excellent.	
	22.11.16		Visited D.A.C.	
	23.11.16		Attended a Horse Show of 176 Infantry Brigade & acted as judge.	
	24.11.16		Visited D.H.Q., Signals & M.M.P.	
	25.11.16		Visited 176 Infantry Brigade group units.	
	26.11.16		Visited 177 Infantry Brigade group units.	
	27.11.16		Visited 178 Infantry Brigade group units.	
	28.11.16		Visited Field Ambulances & Field Coys R.E.	
	29.11.16		Visited No 31 C.C.S. at N.E.S. at LILLE. Four cases Mange occurred in pack work rig. X.H.R.R. Horses & Mules: 36 M.F. stopped. The animals probably became infected through occupation of stables recently vacated by Germans in the area between LILLE & the district of LILLE it is now known Mange existed in German horses. Daily inspection of all animals of these units is being carried out & incontact have been clipped, washed, & isolates. Exercise & work during past week have been light.	

WAR DIARY
or
INTELLIGENCE SUMMARY

(Erase heading not required.)

Army Form C. 2118.

59th (N.M.) Division.   November 1918

Place	Date	Hour	Summary of Events and Information	Remarks and references to Appendices
WATTIGNIES.	30/11/18		Visited new area & new location for M.V.S. at BARLIN (K.24.c.0.3. sheet 44B). There is ample accommodation for men & horses, though a certain amount of repairs to huts is necessary. Visited A.D.V.S. XI Corps at Corps Headquarters & learned that V.E.S. is moving to-day to BETHUNE. It will therefore be necessary to arrange through D.D.V.S. 1st Army for evacuations till we move to new area.	

W.F. Wright. Major
D.A.D.V.S. 59 Division.

59(N.M) Division.

Army Form C. 2118.

WAR DIARY
or
INTELLIGENCE SUMMARY.
(Erase heading not required.)

Dec 1918.

Place	Date	Hour	Summary of Events and Information	Remarks and references to Appendices
WATTIGNIES.	1.12.18		Visited D.D.V.S. V Army at LILLE & learned that nearest V.E.S. to my M.V.S. is at TOURCOING (V. Corps)	
"	2.12.18		Visited 76(N.M) M.V.S.	
"			Visited 176 Infantry Brigade & inspected all units. Condition of 25th Liverpools is very good & coats look well. 17th Royal Dussex—fairly good. 26th R.W.F. fairly good but shoeing of the unit is bad & very backward & I asked D.H.Q. to make arrangements about this.	
"			Visited 178 Infantry Brigade & inspected all units. Condition of 11th R.S.F. excellent, 36th N.F. very good, 13th West Ridings fair & shoeing much neglected. I arranged with OC No 4 Coy A.S.C. to post a farrier temporarily to latter.	
"	3.12.18		Visited & inspected in company with G.O.C., M.V.S., 177 Infantry Brigade units & 20th K.R.R. condition of M.V.S. animals excellent, 76 Durham L.I. & 11 Somerset L.I. good & 16 Essex fairly good. Feet of 11th S.L.I. animals a good deal stumped. 20th K.R.R. fairly good but some feet also stumped. All animals were in good stables mostly empty factories which had previously been used by Germans for a similar purpose. In a few instances there was an insufficiency of ventilation. Asked D.V.S.V Army to collect a horse by motor float from D/295 Brigade R.F.A. at Q.35.C.0.4 (sheet 36) as journey to nearest V.E.S. would be too far for my float.	

(N.M.) DIVISION.

Army Form C. 2118.

WAR DIARY
or
INTELLIGENCE SUMMARY.
(Erase heading not required.)

Instructions regarding War Diaries and Intelligence Summaries are contained in F. S. Regs., Part II. and the Staff Manual respectively. Title pages will be prepared in manuscript.

Place	Date	Hour	Summary of Events and Information	Remarks and references to Appendices
WATTIGNIES.	4.12.18		Visited 2/95 Brigade R.F.A. but found unit had moved to new area.	
"	5.12.18		M.V.S. moved to BARLIN. K33.A.1.5 (Sheet 44B).	
DROUVIN.	6.12.18		Moved my office to DROUVIN. K.H.C. (Sheet 44B)	
"	7.12.18		Visited A.D.V.S. XI Corps at Corps H.Q. Major BAGOT	
BARLIN	8.12.18		Moved my office to BARLIN. Capt Scoby R.A.V.C. took over D.A.D.V.S. duties while proceeds on leave to U/K.	
"	9.12.18		Inspected animals of 1/6 Infantry Brigade Units. Shoeing of the 16th R.W.F. is bad & there are many long feet. Arrangements made for this unit to send its shoeing-smiths & all horses requiring shoeing to No. 2 Coy of 4 Div. Train until further orders.	
"	10.12.18		Visited 54 Sanitary Section at HOUDAIN.	
"	11.12.18		Inspected animals of D.H.Q. M.M.P. & Supple Coy	
"	12.12.18		Inspected animals of 1/2 Pannier A.T. Coy R.E. attached for Veterinary Administration	
"	13.12.18		Inspected animals of 277 A.F.A. attached for Veterinary Administration	
"	14.12.18		Inspected animals & Carriage of 16th R.W.F.	
"	15.12.18		Visited D.H.Q. trade arrangements for the boiling of Linseed Cake.	
"	16.12.18		Inspected animals of 71 (N.M.) Field Ambulance.	

D.A.D.V.S.
594.
(N.Z.) DIVISION.
Army Form C. 2118.
No. 8249/S.V.
Date 1.1.19

WAR DIARY
or
INTELLIGENCE SUMMARY.
(Erase heading not required.)

Instructions regarding War Diaries and Intelligence Summaries are contained in F. S. Regs., Part II. and the Staff Manual respectively. Title pages will be prepared in manuscript.

Place	Date	Hour	Summary of Events and Information	Remarks and references to Appendices
BARLIN	16.12.18		Attended parades at BARLIN & NOEUX-les-MINES for the selection of Brood Mares.	
"	17.12.18		Attended parades at HOUCHIN & ESTREE CAUCHIE for the selection of Brood Mares.	
"	18.12.18		Inspected animals of 20th Liverpools & 20th K.R.R.	
"	19.12.18		Inspected animals of 19th Royal Sussex Regt.	
"	20.12.18		Routine duties in M.V.S.	
"	21.12.18		Visited 464 Field Coy R.E. & 26th R.W.F.	
"	22.12.18		Inspected animals of 71 Field Ambulance at BRUAY	
"	23.12.18		Major Bright D.A.D.V.S. returned from leave.	
DROUVIN	24.12.18		Transferred officer which remained with M.V.S. during my absence to D.H.Q.	
"	25.12.18			
"	26.12.18		Examined animals of D.H.Q. M.M.P. & Signals.	
"	27.12.18		Visited A.D.V.S. XI Corps to discuss the classification of animals for Demobilization purposes. Visited M.V.S.	
"	28.12.18		Commenced Veterinary examinations all animals of Division to classify for Demobilization purposes. Assembled Board consisting of Capt Dooby R.A.V.C., Capt Irwin R.A.V.C. & myself at D.H.Q. & examines 32 animals.	

WAR DIARY
or
INTELLIGENCE SUMMARY.
(Erase heading not required.)

Army Form C. 2118.

Place	Date	Hour	Summary of Events and Information	Remarks and references to Appendices
DROUVIN.	30/12/18		Reassembled Board at D.H.Q. & examined remaining 4 animals of the F&B. All were fit to return to work under the conditions of examination. 11 are for local sales & for destruction. Examined 11 horses of M.M.P. 2 for repatriation & 9 for local sales. Examined 24 animals of Divisional Signal Coy.	
"	31/12/18		Examined 111 animals Divisional Signal Coy completing this unit. Of the total # of 41 animals, 21 are for repatriation, 47 for local sales & 3 for slaughter. Capt. G. Bradley R.A.V.C. proceeded to DUNKIRK on temporary duty with 178 Infantry Brigade.	

W. R. Bright, Major
D.A.D.V.S. 59th Division

Army Form C. 2118.

D.A.D.V.S.
59th
(N.M.) DIVISION.
No. V 49
Date 6/2/19

WAR DIARY
or
INTELLIGENCE SUMMARY.
(Erase heading not required.)

Instructions regarding War Diaries and Intelligence Summaries are contained in F. S. Regs., Part II. and the Staff Manual respectively. Title pages will be prepared in manuscript.

Place	Date	Hour	Summary of Events and Information	Remarks and references to Appendices
	1919			
DROUVIN	1 Jan	-	Veterinary Report. 32 Animals to 7o Field Co. RE. Visited XI Corps HQ to discuss questions arising from Boards.	
"	2 "	"	" 38 " " " " ; 6 animals C.R.E. ; 14 animals Train H.Q. ; 27 animals 25" K.R.R.	
"	3 "	"	" 41 animals 25 K.R.R. ; 35 animals 2.0.0 M.G.Bn	
"	4 "	"	" 150 " " 200" M.G.Bn	
"	5 "	"	" 35 " " ; 19 animals M.V.S.	
"	6 "	"	" 31 " " 295" Bde.R.F.A. H.Q. 2nd section; 140 animals A.R.S. 295" Bde.	
"	7 "	"	" 147 " " B Bty.	
"	8 "	"	" 137 " " C " Capt. J. Bradey R.A.V.C. returned from DUNKIRK	
"	9 "	"	" 149 " " D "	
"	10 "	"	" 209 " " No.1 Sec. 59" D.A.C. ; 33 animals H.Q. 59" D.A.C.	
"	11 "	"	" 205 " " No.2 Sec. " " ; 38 " No.2 Sec. "	
"	12 "	"	" 116 " " S.A.A. " "	
"	13 "	"	" 26 " " H.Q. 296 Bde R.F.A. ; 132 animals A/296 Bde. ; 80 animals B/296 Bde.	
"	14 "	"	" 61 " " B/296 Bde R.F.A. ; 130 " C/296 Bde.	
"	15 "	"	" 146 " " D/296 Bde. R.F.A.	
"	16 "	"	" 29 " " H.Q. 277 A.F.A. Bde. ; 103 " A/277 A.F.A.Bde ; 50 animals B/277 A.F.A.Bde.	

WAR DIARY or INTELLIGENCE SUMMARY

Army Form C. 2118.

January 1919

Place	Date	Hour	Summary of Events and Information	Remarks and references to Appendices
Drouvin	1919 17.1.19	—	Examined Veterinary Board 55 animals B/277 AFA Bde; 144 animals C/277 AFA Bde.	
"	18"	—	" " " 158 " D/277 " 60 " B.A.C./277 Bde	
"	19"	—	" " " 43 " C/277 " Enquired into Remount Officer from MG & 14/2 Field Co.	
"	20"	—	" " " 400 " B.A.C/277 " and Remainder D Bty/277 AFA Bde.	
"	21"	—	" " " 33 "SAA Sn 59" DAC; 4 animals 83" Chinese Labour Coy	
"	22"	—	" " " 141 " No.6 Co. 59 Div Tn; 22 animals No.36 Div Tn; 41 animals 2/3 Field Amb.	
"	23"	—	" " " 9 " CRA	
"	24"	—	Visited XI Corps V.E.S. & M.V.S. Arranging disposal Butchery animals.	
"	25"	—	295" Bde RFA, MVS and ADVS XI Corps re arranged evacuation of a number of cases/male.	
"	26"	—	Capt. G.G. Scott proceeded on leave to England; left H.W. Deane took temporary command of MVS.	
"	27"	—	Examined animals of DHQ, AMP, & 59 Signals.	
"	28"	—	Malleins " " " ; Visited MVS; Visited 176 POW camp to investigate outbreak of Mange	
"	29"	—	G.O.C. inspected MVS; attended	
"	30"	—	Visited 296" Bde RFA. Inspected sick with V.O.	
"	31"	—	295" " " " "	
"	"	—	MVS	

W.F. Bright
Major
DADVS 59 Div

59th (N.M) Division

Feby 1919.

WAR DIARY
or
INTELLIGENCE SUMMARY.
(Erase heading not required.)

Army Form C. 2118

Place	Date	Hour	Summary of Events and Information	Remarks and references to Appendices
TROUVIN.	1.2.19		Visited office A.D.V.S. XI Corps.	
"	2.2.19		Inspected animals of P.H.R. M.M.P. & Signals.	
"	3.2.19		Routine duties in office.	
"	4.2.19		Took over duties of A.D.V.S. XI Corps in addition to my present ones.	
"	5.2.19		Visited XI Corps V.E.S. BETHUNE & 2/1 (N.M) M.V.S. BARLIN.	
"	6.2.19		At XI Corps Headquarters doing duties of A.D.V.S.	
"	7.2.19		"	
"	8.2.19		"	
"	9.2.19		"	
"	10.2.19		"	
"	11.2.19		"	
"	12.2.19		"	
"	13.2.19		"	
"	14.2.19		"	
"	15.2.19		Visited ARRAS to arrange sales of animals.	
"	16.2.19		In office of A.D.V.S. XI Corps. Compiling A.F.A. 2000.	

D.A.D.V.S.
(M.D.) DIVISION.

Army Form C. 2118.

WAR DIARY
or
INTELLIGENCE SUMMARY.
(Erase heading not required.)

Instructions regarding War Diaries and Intelligence Summaries are contained in F. S. Regs., Part II. and the Staff Manual respectively. Title pages will be prepared in manuscript.

Place	Date	Hour	Summary of Events and Information	Remarks and references to Appendices
PROUVIN	17.2.19		Duties at office A.D.V.S. XI Corps. Capt J. BRADLEY, R.A.V.C. attached 296 Brigade R.F.A. died.	
"	18.2.19		Visited ST POL to arrange Sales of animals.	
"	19.2.19		Went to ARRAS to arrange Horse Sales. Proceeded from there to 1st Army H.Q. at VALENCIENNES to confer with D.D.V.S. 1st Army.	
"	19.2.19		Returned with D.D.V.S. 1st Army to XI Corps & Division. Proceeded with D.D.V.S. 1st to 63rd Battery 189 Brigade to investigate Epizootic Lymphangitis outbreak.	
"	20.2.19		Visited FREVENT to arrange sale details. Visited XI Corps H.Q.	
"	21.2.19		Duties at office of A.D.V.S. XI Corps. Visited ST POL to arrange Horse Sales.	
"	22.2.19		Visited 7(K.M) M.V.S. Handed over duties to A.D.V.S. XI Corps & advised him in office.	
"	23.2.19		Routine duties at Division.	
"	24.2.19		Visited M.V.S. & 76.1 Coy Divisional Train.	
"	25.2.19		Visited 295 Brigade R.F.A. Routine duties in office.	
"	26.2.19		Visited 296 Brigade R.F.A.	
"	27.2.19		Routine duties at office.	
"	28.2.19		Routine duties at office.	

6 F Bright Major.
D.A.D.V.S. 59th Division.

D.A.D.V.S.
59th (N.M.) Division

Army Form C.2118.
No. 166.V

WAR DIARY
or
INTELLIGENCE SUMMARY.
(Erase heading not required.)

59th (N.M) Division
March 1919.

Place	Date	Hour	Summary of Events and Information	Remarks and references to Appendices
DROUVIN.	1.3.19		Visited office of A.D.V.S. XI Corps.	
"	2.3.19		Routine duties at office.	
"	3.3.19		Visited Corps Heavy Artillery, DIVION, to complete sale papers for 50 animals to be sold on the 4th inst.	
"	4.3.19		Attended a sale of animals at BRUAY, 150 "Z" animals from this Division & 50 animals from Corps Heavy Artillery.	
"	5.3.19		Visited Corps H.Q. & took over temporarily duties of A.D.V.S. XI Corps in addition to my own.	
"	6.3.19		Move of Division to CALAIS-DUNKERQUE area commenced.	
"	7.3.19		M.V.S. moved to AIRE en route to CALAIS area.	
CALAIS.	8.3.19		Moved my Office to BEAUMARAIS Camp CALAIS. M.V.S. moved to SERQUE en route to CALAIS area.	
"	9.3.19		M.V.S. arrived at BALINGHEM (CALAIS area).	
"	10.3.19		Visited No. 4 Veterinary Hospital.	
"	11.3.19		Duties in office. Capt. H.S. Davies, R.A.V.C. proceeded on leave to ENGLAND.	
"	12.3.19		Duties in office.	
"	13.3.19		Visited Australian No. 4 Veterinary Hospital in company with G.O.C. Division.	
"	14.3.19		Routine duties in office. Recommended the breaking up of M.V.S. & D.D.V.S. Northern as they are no longer required.	

Army Form C. 2118.

WAR DIARY
or
INTELLIGENCE SUMMARY.
(Erase heading not required.)

Instructions regarding War Diaries and Intelligence Summaries are contained in F.S. Regs., Part II. and the Staff Manual respectively. Title pages will be prepared in manuscript.

Place	Date	Hour	Summary of Events and Information	Remarks and references to Appendices
CALAIS	15.3.19		Routine duties in office.	
"	16.3.19		Visited 16th Veterinary Hospital.	
"	17.3.19		Visited M.V.S. Closed my office in preparation for my departure from Division.	
"	18.3.19		Left Division to join 3rd Division. It is understood that it is not intended to continue the appointment of a D.A.D.V.S. to 5yl Division.	

W. Farewright. Major.
D.A.D.V.S. 5y Divn.

www.ingramcontent.com/pod-product-compliance
Lightning Source LLC
Chambersburg PA
CBHW081442160426
43193CB00013B/2353